What people are saying

# Us

"Dan Tocchini understands the subtle turns of mind, soul, and will that move people toward or away from 'Us' in marriage. Follow his explanations and illustrations closely and apply them in your life."

**Dallas Willard,** best-selling author of *The Divine Conspiracy* and professor of philosophy, University of Southern California

"It is now a truism: We live in a culture that is good at helping people plan a wedding, but bad at helping people plan a marriage. *Us* shows us how to achieve a rewarding marriage by rewarding it with mystery and miracle."

**Leonard Sweet,** author of *So Beautiful, AquaChurch 2.0,* and the upcoming *Nudge*

"This is a book about how to make a marriage work. It will force you to seek God, humble yourself, and get real; it's not a book for cowards. Dan Tocchini will guide you into effective ways to communicate with your spouse. No matter the state of your marriage, this book can show you how to repair and improve your relationship with the person you love the most. *Us: A User's Guide* will give you hope for a future in God and with each other. Prepare to work hard."

**J. R. Young,** executive director, Law Enforcement Chaplaincy Service, Sonoma County

# A USER'S GUIDE

# DANIEL L. TOCCHINI

transforming lives together

US
Published by David C. Cook
4050 Lee Vance View
Colorado Springs, CO 80918 U.S.A.

David C. Cook Distribution Canada
55 Woodslee Avenue, Paris, Ontario, Canada N3L 3E5

David C. Cook U.K., Kingsway Communications
Eastbourne, East Sussex BN23 6NT, England

David C. Cook and the graphic circle C logo
are registered trademarks of Cook Communications Ministries.

The Web site addresses recommended throughout this book are offered as a
resource to you. These Web sites are not intended in any way to be or imply an
endorsement on the part of David C. Cook, nor do we vouch for their content.

Some of the names in this book have been changed
to protect the privacy of the individuals.

All Scripture quotations, unless otherwise noted, are taken from the *Holy Bible,
New International Version*. *NIV*. Copyright © 1973, 1978, 1984 by International
Bible Society. Used by permission of Zondervan. All rights reserved. Scripture
quotations marked msg are taken from *THE MESSAGE*. Copyright © by Eugene
H. Peterson 1993, 1994, 1995, 1996, 2000, 2001, 2002. Used by permission of
NavPress Publishing Group; nlt are taken from the New Living Translation of
the Holy Bible. New Living Translation copyright © 1996, 2004 by Tyndale
Charitable Trust. Used by permission of Tyndale House Publishers; nkjv are taken
from the New King James Version. Copyright © 1982 by Thomas Nelson, Inc.
Used by permission. All rights reserved; net are from the NET Bible® Copyright
© 1996-2006 by Biblical Studies Press L.L.C. www.bible.org. All rights reserved; esv
are taken from The Holy Bible, English Standard Version. Copyright © 2000; 2001
by Crossway Bibles, a division of Good News Publishers. Used by permission. All
rights reserved. kjv are taken from the King James Version of the Bible. (Public
Domain.) Italics in Scripture have been added by author for emphasis.

LCCN 2009938923
ISBN 978-1-4347-6473-7
eISBN 978-1-4347-0082-7

© 2010 Dan Tocchini
Published in association with the literary agency of Esther Fedorkevich, Fedd &
Company, Inc. Literary Agency, 9759 Concord Pass, Brentwood, TN 37027.

The Team: Terry Behimer, Brian Thomasson, Amy Gregory,
Sarah Schultz, Jaci Schneider, and Karen Athen
Cover Design: Amy Kiechlin

Printed in the United States of America
First Edition 2010

1 2 3 4 5 6 7 8 9 10

102909

To my mother, Jeannette Destruel Tocchini, who showed me that love always wins

# CONTENTS

Foreword

# Dwelling in Beulah Land

It is now a truism: We live in a culture that is good at helping people plan a wedding, but bad at helping people plan a marriage. But the above truism that inspired this powerful book you are now holding— and makes Dan Tocchini's *Us* so valuable a resource—has one problem. Can you "plan" a marriage? Really? You can plan a wedding. But can you plan, or only prepare, for a marriage? I suspect the latter.

You can only live a marriage. You can only experience and embrace what Tocchini calls "a rewarding marriage," or what an old hymn based on Isaiah 62:4–5 calls "Dwelling in Beulah Land." The Hebrew word for "marriage" is *Beulah*. A Beulah Land relationship, a rewarding marriage, requires some rewording and some rewanding.

First, some rewording. The two most important phrases to learn in Beulah Land are comprised of five words: (1) "Say more" and (2) "Maybe you're right."

(1) "Say more": When you don't understand what you've just heard, or when you don't know what to say next, or when you're tempted to say something you know you'll later regret, these are the only words that should come out of your mouth: "Say more."

(2) "Maybe you're right": Robert Fass photographed and interviewed thirty-seven couples married for at least forty years. Fass turned up this nugget of wisdom about the secret to a long, successful marriage. The three words that save a marriage are not "I love you," Fass reveals in his book *As Long As We Both Shall Live* (2008). They are "Maybe you're right."

If I can reword one more time, let me be bold and suggest a different word for Beulah Land than marriage. I don't expect this other word to catch on. I don't expect other people to run out and start using it. But I do want to propose a reword for *marriage*.

The word *marriage* comes from food culture, where cooks "marry" ingredients. When you marry two flavors, each one loses its identity, and a new creation is born. That's why when the marriage candle was first introduced into wedding ceremonies, the bride and the groom extinguished their individual candles and only let the marriage candle burn.

But as Tocchini shows in the unforgettable characters in this book—Mark and Rene, Rey and Enid, Len and Sara, Malcolm and Eva, Karl and Millie, and yes, even Dan and Aileen (the author and his wife)—every person God created is unique, a one-of-a-kind unrepeatable who shouldn't be any other way than they are. Part of the problem with *marriage* is that one loses their identity in the other, or the words some brides use to calm down during the procession become the motto of the marriage: "aisle … altar … him." Do we really want to get married like flour and butter get married and become a roux, no longer flour and no longer butter?

There is another word and metaphor from food culture that better suggests to me what it means to "dwell in Beulah Land."

That word is *marinate*. When you marinate ingredients, something very different happens than when you marry ingredients. The process of marinating is to bring two distinct ingredients together, not so that they can lose themselves in each other, but so that each one becomes more distinctive, more unique, while at the same time the two together create a magical third, a *tertium quid*. Take the best marinade and the worst steak, and you get the best steak if you soak and ferment and saturate the two ingredients long enough.

In Beulah Land, people enter into a lifelong covenant that is less about marrying each other than marinating each other. Two lives are so saturated and steeped in each others' uniqueness and particularity that each one's distinctiveness is drawn out and deepened, while at the same time a magical, mysterious, even mystical third presence is conceived in the knowing of knowing. Marriage is an amusement park that you exit as soon as the fun comes to a stop. Marinating is a relationship you believe in enough to stick around until the fun returns. In Beulah Land, a marriage is marinated in heaven.

You see why it won't catch on? Will anyone look into the eyes of a lover and say, "Will you marinate me?" Plus, marinating takes too long. Marrying is over in a moment. Marinating takes a lifetime.

We're into microwave marriages. We're into crock-pot marriages. We're into crack-pot marriages built on all sorts of craziness and crazed foundations. We're even into Pol-Pot marriages, where two people are bonded together by constant fighting (named after Pol-Pot, during whose three-year reign one-fifth of the population of Cambodia perished). Worst of all, we're into what Tocchini calls "consumer marriages" rather than "kingdom marriages."

There are many things I shall never forget about *Us*: the connection between the original meanings of *sin* and *character*; the "Len" story with the gotcha ending; the shift in our relational thinking from rehabilitation to reinvention; the "nerd list"; Dan's divorced mother toasting her ex's young wife. But most of all, its case studies linked to biblical stories promise a rewarding marriage by doing more than rewording it. *Us* shows us how to achieve a rewarding marriage by rewanding it with magic and mystery and miracle.

Leonard Sweet,
author of *So Beautiful, AquaChurch
2.0*, and the upcoming *Nudge*

He came to those who knew the
language, but they did not respond. Those
who did became a new creation (his children),
they read the signs and responded.
These children were born out of sharing in
the creative activity of God. They heard the
conversation still going on, here, now, and
took part, discovering a new
way of being people.
To be invited to share in a conversation
about the nature of life, was for them, a glorious
opportunity not to be missed.

*John 1:11–14*

# WELCOME TO US

I hope those words from John's gospel take hold of you. They're not the same ones you put to memory as a grade-schooler in Sunday school. This translation was brought to life by Professor Clive Scott, who wrote it based on what the Reformation-era scholar Erasmus had rendered in the sixteenth century. And, like everything else in this book, I hope it gets your attention and leads you to question your assumptions about you, your spouse, and especially your marriage.

Perhaps you find yourself like those among the first-century Jews who "knew the language," but didn't know quite how to respond. Perhaps you never realized that God has truly "invited you into a conversation," thinking instead that He was simply looking for your tacit acknowledgment.

And beyond all this, I'm almost certain that you never imagined what any of this has to do with your marriage. This is not your typical marriage book in that it's not really designed to simply enhance your marriage and make it better. It's more like a fresh introduction to you, together. To *Us*. It's more like a, well … *User's Guide,* daring you and your spouse to join in the "conversation still going on," rather than banging your heads on the same old walls:

"We're not intimate anymore."

"She always nags me."

"He never talks to me."

"We've drifted so far apart."

Do any of these complaints sound familiar? Since you are reading this book, chances are that you can relate to at least one of these statements. It is no secret that happy, lasting marriages are an anomaly in today's culture, but it doesn't have to be that way. We don't have to be doomed by historical statistics about the rise in divorce and the decline of fulfilling unions. Marriage—your marriage—can be reborn if you are willing. Are you ready to learn how?

Even if you are only thinking about getting married or you and your partner are working well at this time, this book is still a useful guide to creating and maintaining a strong and healthy relationship. It may even help prevent some of the problems I talk about from creeping up!

*Us* is a transformational approach to breaking through the barriers and getting out of the ruts in your marriage by paying attention to, talking about, listening to, and exploring conversations married partners rarely entertain because they represent possible conflict, chaos, and disruption. Instead of talking about these things, we tend to hide them, avoid them, or simply pretend they don't exist.

Just as Adam and Eve shrank away from the Master Gardener in shame, we impair what God wants to create in our marriage by carrying on in our belief that we know a better way than His. Meanwhile the fear and uncertainty created by these elephants in the room grow like fungus and ultimately sabotage our relationship. Not only that, but we begin to despair and remain confused about whether or not a rewarding marriage is even possible. In *that* moment our marriage is wobbling on very shaky ground.

By talking about such deep and difficult issues, we can begin to open the door for intimacy with our spouse as well as develop a greater dependency on God. If we take the step toward loving out loud and continue to walk in the light of truth, God will reconcile our pains, hurts, and fears. He can take our damaging conversational wars and turn them into new and unprecedented possibilities for romance, passion, intimacy, and love. He will transform chaos into order and bring beauty to our messes.

The problem often is that we are drawn too deep into our own selves to even care about what a beyond-our-imagination marriage can look like. Marriage, much like our consumer culture, has become a me-me-me game that we play to win. Our inner nature tells us that we must strive to be comfortable, be in control, be right, or look and feel good. This pull is so strong and so seductive that we use whatever strategy we can, and at whatever cost, to maintain these "needs." But the cost can be great. Often it comes in the form of signing divorce papers.

*Us* exposes the tendency we have to be swayed by the consumer culture that only leads to an unfulfilled and broken marriage. Living marriage according to His kingdom is the antidote for our culture's deadly whispers to live life selfishly and impulsively for immediate and temporary satisfaction.

As you read these pages, please notice what is stirred in you. If you find yourself angry, agitated, sad, lonely, excited, elated, or numb, take some time to pray and meditate about what is happening to you. Ask yourself the question, "What has so powerfully provoked me?" Be willing to reconsider your long-held assumptions about your spouse and about marriage itself as you read this *User's Guide*.

Although I've included some writing space throughout the book, you will probably want to write in a separate journal so you can keep a record of your inner experiences, especially if you plan to eventually share this book with your spouse or someone else. Take the time to explore what you are going through. I can assure you it will aid the transformation of your marriage and can change you and your spouse's lives.

The disciplines of praying, fasting, and meditating are powerful ways to catch hold of desires that often undermine your ability to love your spouse the way you would want them to love you. Practicing these disciplines as you read this book and working through some of the assignments will prove to be valuable as you aim to walk into the broken places of your marriage.

*Us* isn't a systematic approach to marriage. It is a very clear invitation for a couple to develop a relationship with God, life, and themselves by practicing the art and science of conversing. While so many marriage books focus on fixing your relationship in three or thirty steps, my commitment is to provide more than a system of steps and principles. In this book you will find a way of relating that can open the possibility of entering into a future worth having with your spouse, regardless of the trying circumstances you may (and probably will) face.

Be open to a new future in your marriage. Be open to transformation. Be open to God bringing the new into your relationship.

Now close your eyes and imagine yourselves meeting each other for the very first time, just as Adam and Eve did. Begin to think of your spouse as a whole new person to explore, to walk with, to enjoy! Think of your spouse as a unique and perfect gift given to you by the Creator with no strings attached.

My friend, get ready to let go of the old and experience the new.

## Chapter One

# THE CONSUMER VS. THE KINGDOM

*The significant problems we face cannot
be solved at the same level of thinking
we were at when we created them.*

*Albert Einstein*

This book is about challenging the marriage assumptions that have prevented you from seeing new possibilities in the uncharted waters of *Us.* The first assumption that simply must go is that you or your spouse needs to change in order for your marriage to improve.

As difficult as it may seem, I want you to consider the possibility that nothing about you or your spouse needs to change.

Nothing at all.

Beyond this I ask you to consider the reason that you began thinking that one of you needed to change. Could it be that you have unwittingly embraced the consumerism of our culture and applied it to your precious wife? Your precious husband? Such that you began to think of that person as a commodity? That's exactly where Mark and Rene were when they came to see me. (I should mention that there are times couples are counseled by me and my wife, Aileen. We do this on an as-needed basis.)

Mark and Rene, a forty-something couple with fifteen years of marriage under their belts, spewed venom back and forth at each other during our marriage coaching session. The verbal onslaught was tough to listen to, even though I've worked with hundreds of couples and heard it all.

Mark furrowed his brows, glared at his wife, and then looked at me. "You know, Dan, I can't stand being married to Rene any longer! If I had known this marriage was going to be like this, I never would have gotten married. Now we have four children and I feel like I'm trapped!" Mark's rage bubbled over. It was obvious he was purposely trying to hurt his wife with his words.

Rene looked disgusted. "Married? Really? You really believe we're married? If that's true, you don't act like it at all!" She spoke with contempt in her voice. "For starters you have a girlfriend in New Mexico. If you think you can continue to carry on with that woman, I want a divorce."

Mark escalated the attack. "Well, you drove me to her. She pays attention to me when I'm around and actually cares about what I do. All you do is gripe at me for not being enough. Besides, you kicked me out, so what am I supposed to do? Just wait around until you feel like inviting me back home?"

I was silent and let them duke it out with their words for a bit. I knew exactly where this conversation was going.

In a soft voice, as tears dripped down her cheeks, Rene turned to me. "Dan, I just got tired of waiting for him to do the things he said he would do." Then she whipped her head around and faced her husband. "When you were home with us, you would get up early in the morning and go to the office, where you worked all day with women. Then, while I was stuck at home with the kids, you would go out to dinner with them. I got tired of feeling abandoned and so I decided since you were never home and always out with other women, we might as well make it official. That's why I kicked you out. I hoped that you would soon realize what you had lost and begin to court me again. That never happened. You seemed glad to have left. Anyway, even while you were here, there wasn't an ounce of romance left in our marriage! How do you think that makes me feel? I want a man who will put me first in his life. Honestly, Mark, when we first met twenty years ago, I believed you were that man, but now I don't even know you."

Mark bristled and took a deep breath, doing his best to maintain some semblance of composure. "Dan, I'm in the fashion business. Most of the people I work with are either gay men or women. I can't help that! Why can't Rene support me? After all, I'm the one who provides a great home and pays for the kids' private school, the medical care, food, clothing—geez, nobody has had to go without anything. I wasn't seeing anybody until I realized that I just couldn't go on like that any longer. I was beginning to feel like a hermit. All Rene was doing was getting back at me for what she felt I owed her. When she kicked me out, I got an apartment and, sure, a girlfriend on the side. But I needed a companion, somebody who made me feel like I mattered. I just couldn't take the nagging and complaining anymore!"

Rene turned away so that Mark couldn't see her cry. Then she said something I'm sure many of you either say yourself or hear from your spouse.

"But what about me, Mark? What about my needs?"

It was the classic "I-need-I-need-I-need" complaint. Yet each one was only listening to their own needs.

The frustrating part for me was that Mark and Rene had the tools they needed to turn their marriage around. It wasn't like they didn't know what they needed to do. Though I had worked with them for about two years, they were not getting anywhere. If there was any chance of this marriage not ending in divorce, one thing needed to happen.

They needed to renew their thinking.

Specifically, Mark and Rene had to come to a transformation of how they viewed their marriage. It had nothing to do with changing their behavior or actions toward themselves and each other. Change in that sense is superficial and many times it is temporary. God has called us to rely on Him, not for changing even what we consider "wrong" with us or bad, but in how we relate to God, ourselves, and each other, as well as what we cannot change. We don't need to change, fix, or better the bad stuff about us; we need the kind of change we call transformation—changing how we view ourselves, our spouse, and our marriage. In other words, the way you view your spouse or a particular situation you are in—whether you are fighting again about the same thing you fought about yesterday, or your kids are rebelling in the worst way, or there has been betrayal—is what determines the quality of your life together.

This is what Mark and Rene needed to do. They had to look at their union in a completely new way. If this didn't happen, all the tools and applications and skills they had learned to save their marriage would be useless. Why? Because they had begun to view one another as products—something they thought needed to be different or better. Therefore they would use those tools, applications, and skills to try and "fix" what they thought needed to change, like a defective product, radically distracting them from what could be new without having to fix anything. In fact, if you pay close attention to the language they use, it is not much different than the language we might use when researching a purchase. It was time for them to stop tallying their expenses and start counting the cost.

Luke writes how Jesus was once followed by a large crowd. Jesus tells these folks something very powerful about what it really means to follow Christ and His kingdom.

> *Anyone who comes to me but refuses to let go of father, mother, spouse, children, brothers, sisters—yes, even one's own self!—can't be my disciple. Anyone who won't shoulder his own cross and follow behind me can't be my disciple. Is there anyone here who, planning to build a new house, doesn't first sit down and figure the cost so you'll know if you can complete it? If you only get the foundation laid and then run out of money, you're going to look pretty foolish. Everyone passing by will poke fun at you: "He started something he couldn't finish." Luke 14:25–30 MSG)*

Jesus was saying that before we even consider getting into relationship with Him, we need to count the cost. He clarified His statement by specifying that the potential cost could be loss of familial affections and those close to us, as well as the death of the traditions and habits that are a part of these relationships. Jesus pulled no punches. The cost is great.

Marriage is one of God's tools for building His kingdom, and if we are to pioneer the possibility of a kingdom life together, we must prepare to make life-defining sacrifices. We must prepare to change the way we view life or change our purpose for living together.

This call doesn't make any sense when it comes to our culture. Why? Because we live in a "consumer"-oriented culture. It is a part of who we are because it is what we were born into. Our relationships in particular, are immersed in consumerism.

A consumer views marriage as if it exists for individual fulfillment. If a spouse isn't being fulfilled, then that "consumer" looks for another relationship or even falls into an addiction to fulfill their particular needs—whether to look good, feel good, be right, or be in control. Mark and Rene's marriage is a prime example of a consumer marriage. Remember some of their complaints?

Mark talked about his reason for dating a woman in New Mexico. He said, "I needed a companion, somebody who made me feel like I mattered. I just couldn't take the nagging, whining, and complaining!" Mark wanted to feel good by being appreciated and not be asked to live up to what he had promised. He also wanted to be right and in control, so he used his interpretation of Rene's asking him to move out as a way to justify his going out with the other woman.

Rene remarked, "I got tired of feeling abandoned and so I decided since you were never home and always out with other women, we might as well make it official. That's why I kicked you out. I hoped that you would soon realize what you had lost and begin to court me again." She also wanted to feel good and be in control. She longed to be romanced, and her way to control that outcome was to kick her husband out.

Notice the price Mark and Rene were willing to pay to manipulate the other to get what they wanted—the looming dissolution of their marriage. Many Christian couples approach marriage this same way, as a consumer, because they don't know or understand what God intended marriage to be.

## AND NOW FOR SOMETHING COMPLETELY DIFFERENT

Mark and Rene had entered the death spiral of the consumer marriage. For all their talk about their "needs," they were missing their real need: a new way of understanding what marriage is all about for them as citizens of the kingdom of Jesus.

Jesus steps on the scene and says, "Where's My kingdom in all of this? Your personal fulfillment and satisfaction are the means to the end. There's nothing temporary about your marriage, and it is not disposable. You stick with each other and work diligently to develop your oneness, even if it is deeply dissatisfying and unfulfilling for long periods of time. Abandon your consumer-marriage mindset and come and follow Me. I will train you in how to stick with something and not be stuck with it!"

I don't have a program to prescribe, or a list of marriage pointers to post on the fridge. I want you to enter something completely new, together. Set the past aside. Don't even look back there, not even as a frame of reference. What I'm offering is total transformation, something truly, completely new. Something unprecedented, unparalleled.

## SURRENDERING CERTITUDE

The question before us is, will we take Jesus up on His offer or will we allow our precious marriages—our families for generations to come—to go down with the ship of the consumer mindset? Let's focus in and look at the difference between the two types of marriages in greater detail.

The consumer marriage says, "I will be who I ought to be as long as, and to the degree, that you are who you ought to be." The kingdom marriage says, "I will be who I ought to be whether you are or not."

If you are anything like me, you're probably asking, "Why would I be who I ought to be if the other person is taking (or may take) advantage of me?" or "Why should I change if my spouse doesn't (or may not) want to change?" or "Why should I do all the work if my spouse doesn't (or may not) want to work just as hard as I am?" These questions are all grounded in the fear of the unknown, which is a huge part of consumer thinking.

Here is what I mean: The one thing we as consumers want from products is predictability. We want to know exactly what we will get, how they will work, who will be delivering them, when they will arrive, and how much they will cost. In short we want to have as much control as we can possibly get, with the most efficiency and convenience possible. Anything outside of that is unknown, uncertain, and definitely uncomfortable. Therefore we strive to maintain control at all costs and eliminate any risks of encountering or dealing with the unknown.

Surely it is no accident that because of our innate need for this type of certitude, God calls those of us who desire to be united with another to be married. This union, in His eyes, depends on submission instead of control. In marriage, when we submit to the unknown, we become open to the rewarding depths of its mysteries. One of my favorite passages about this concept is found in Ephesians and is a pictorial example of a kingdom marriage that counters the consumer lifestyle.

> *Out of respect for Christ, be courteously reverent to one another.*

> *Wives, understand and support your husbands in ways that show your support for Christ. The husband provides leadership to his wife the way Christ does to his church, not by domineering but by cherishing. So just as the church submits to Christ as he exercises such leadership, wives should likewise submit to their husbands.*

> *Husbands, go all out in your love for your wives, exactly as Christ did for the church—a love marked by giving, not getting. Christ's love makes the church whole. His words evoke her beauty. Everything he does and says is designed to bring the best out of her, dressing her in*

*dazzling white silk, radiant with holiness. And that is*
*how husbands ought to love their wives. They're really*
*doing themselves a favor—since they're already "one"*
*in marriage.*

*No one abuses his own body, does he? No, he feeds and*
*pampers it. That's how Christ treats us, the church,*
*since we are part of his body. And this is why a man*
*leaves father and mother and cherishes his wife. No*
*longer two, they become "one flesh." (Eph. 5:21–31*
*MSG)*

What strikes me most when I read this Scripture is the way
Christ treats the church—through loving, honoring, respecting, and
giving. This illustrates for us the manner that each husband is to
treat his wife and how each wife is to honor her husband. Paul's
commission to us powerfully aligns with Jesus' words in Luke about
counting the cost. In both passages we are called to submission. If we
want to be Jesus' disciples, we must submit to Him and follow His
example. If our marriage is to be a blessing to us and our community,
we must submit to each other.

While our culture has taught us that the highest reward is
to be served and be the master of our own destiny, we are told
something contrary in the Bible. God reminds us that the greatest
value in life is to submit and give ourselves over to God and one
another. Becoming a servant will bring forth a greater blessing than
this consumer world could ever give us. As it relates to marriage,
submission is an opposing force to certitude, our need to be in

control, and our belief that we know everything. The bottom line is that being a know-it-all is an obstacle to embracing mystery in marriage.

Think about this: Do we know everything about God? Of course not. Actually, the one thing we can be certain about is how inexhaustible the mystery of God is, as declared in the book of Job.

> *Do you think you can explain the mystery of God? Do you think you can diagram God Almighty? God is far higher than you can imagine, far deeper than you can comprehend, stretching farther than earth's horizons, far wider than the endless ocean. If he happens along, throws you in jail then hauls you into court, can you do anything about it? He sees through vain pretensions, spots evil a long way off—no one pulls the wool over his eyes! Hollow men, hollow women, will wise up about the same time mules learn to talk. (Job 11:7–12* MSG)

The foundation of life is God, and He has revealed Himself as mystery. This characteristic and the way He has invited us to discover and experience who He is reflects the very nature of mystery inherent in marriage. When we abandon our certitude and instead submit to God and then to one another, we open the door to the possibility of continual renewal. We stop pigeonholing ourselves, our spouse, and our marriage into what we think we know about them. And it is only by embracing mystery that we can begin to experience a transformational kingdom marriage.

POSSIBILITIES?

One night Mark showed up at my house with steam pouring out of his ears. It was obvious he was desperate. "Dan, I need to talk to you. I can't take Rene's nagging any longer. All she wants to do is try and control me. She is so insecure that I can't stand being with her! I can't do this anymore. It's over."

Frankly I was taken aback by his certitude about where Rene was coming from, so I asked him how he knew she was insecure. For the next hour Mark and I talked about that supposed surety. Mark also remarked that there was more bad than good in the marriage.

I reminded him about the "for better or for worse" part he uttered in their marriage vows and asked, "Isn't that what you promised her? That you would stick around for better or for worse?"

Mark thought for a moment and said, "Sure, but she just won't submit to me!" (Ah, spoken like a true consumer. I have heard this same thing from so many people of faith.)

After talking with him a bit, I learned that many of Mark's Christian friends thought Rene was rebellious. I asked him to consider another point of view. I brought up the passage in Ephesians about submission and asked him what level of submission men are called to.

Mark replied confidently, "We are to be the head of the family!"

"Actually," I pointed out, "it says we are to love our wives as Jesus loves the church and gave Himself as a sacrifice for her. My question to you is, if we are to love our wives as Jesus loves the church, who actually gave themselves first—Jesus or the church?"

"Jesus did," Mark said in low tones.

"And who was crucified for the church to see her resurrected?"

"Jesus was."

"The Bible says Jesus' love was 'marked by giving not getting,' yet when we talk about your relationship with Rene," I said, "you dwell on what you are not getting. I wonder how anybody would tend to feel if they were constantly reminded of their insufficiencies."

"I get your point," Mark retorted. "But the bottom line still is that all she does is gripe."

I probed further. "Are you certain that is all she does?"

"Okay, not all the time. I know it isn't healthy to use the words *always* and *never*, but she does it most of the time!"

I asked Mark if he was certain what Rene was doing was complaining. Could she in fact be doing something else that he was not able to see because he was so blinded by what he was so sure he knew?

Mark thought about what I said for a moment and then looked at me. "I am so tired of this relationship and how hard it is to just connect on anything. I think I just want to be done with it."

I paused for a minute, weighing my response. "Mark, I do get you are being honest about how it feels for you, but do you think your certainty that the relationship is what you have described has anything to do with your despair? I mean, if Rene is who you are certain she is, and there is no possibility that she could be any other way, then I understand your despair. But what if things were *not* exactly the way you have them set in your head? Would it matter? If there was another possibility, would you like to know about it?"

"Yes, I would want to know if I am missing something." Mark let out a frustrated sigh. "But it just doesn't seem worth the time!"

"According to who? You? Rene? Your kids?" I asked with an edge in my voice.

"You're right. I guess there can't be much possibility if I am so certain about who she is, how she will respond, what she says, and what she wants."

(Bingo!)

"Mark, what if the loss of your romance for Rene had little to nothing to do with her?" I inquired.

A look of surprise came over his face and he inquired, "What do you mean?"

"If you think you know who she is, what she will say and think, as well as how she will react, then there are no new possibilities available. There is no mystery in the relationship and therefore no sense of anticipation for what God may be doing between you. No mystery equals no romance!"

"Perhaps that has something to do with the despair I'm feeling," Mark mused.

I wondered out loud and asked, "Do you think seeing Jennifer contributes to that sense of despair?"

"Why would you say that?"

"It seems obvious to me that the more you see her, the more you will need to be right about these judgments you have about Rene so you can justify seeing Jennifer. That way you don't have to be open to who you and Rene can be together. But sooner or later, Mark, you will have to explain this to your children. The costs are huge for the few fleeting moments of self-satisfaction you are gaining with Jennifer. Now that is a real formula for despair."

Mark sat still for a few moments and then came back strong. "All this wondering about my certitude about Rene seems like a waste of time. I have been with her for fifteen years. I really do feel like I know how she will react."

"Mark, I am asking you to consider and explore what you are making up about her reaction. When she complains about things, do you investigate her complaint? Have you stopped and wondered what she is trying to communicate by her complaining?"

His answer was immediate. "Yes. She is trying to control me because she is insecure."

"Are you certain she is insecure? Perhaps part of submitting to another is being open to who your spouse is outside of your prejudice of them. I know you have your historical evidence to validate your judgment of why Rene reacts the way she does, but how much time have you spent questioning that certainty?"

Mark still wasn't fazed. "Dan, you don't understand what it is like to live with her and her nagging. She doesn't care and I don't see any good that could come out of this. This is just too much suffering to have to go through."

I made one last attempt. "Mark, you know the suffering Aileen and I have gone through in our marriage, right?"

He nodded in acknowledgment while I reminded him of my story. "My wife and I were discussing divorce and were separated in our own house for a year. We saw no possibility that we would ever care enough for each other to ever be intimate again. But we decided that our son deserved the chance of us trying. We needed to at least try and trust God. We needed to at least try to devote some time to exploring our own judgments of each other. We needed to at least try and understand where the other was coming from outside of the record of wrongs we had built up to bolster our judgments of each other.

"Our hope and prayer was that God would somehow draw us into some new possibilities for each other. We realized we had loved one another once before. We experienced great passion for one another, much like you and Rene have shared in the past. We kept believing that God would open possibility in the suffering if we were willing to love each other as we wanted the other to love us. We were determined to get out of the consumer mindset that had done nothing except ruin our marriage."

Something hit home. Mark promised to think about it and we ended the conversation.

Mark needed to abandon the what's-in-it-for-me mentality and discard his certitude about Rene's feelings, thoughts, and actions. He needed to embrace the possibility that could emerge from exploring the mystery of who she is and who they could be together.

I know this because this is what saved my marriage. I gave mystery a chance. The second I was able to allow mystery to seep into my thought process about my wife … the second I was able to admit that perhaps I didn't know what she was thinking or the reasons for how she would react to particular things … the second I was able to allow God to intervene and transform my heart to give without expecting … was the second that the possibility opened for transforming our relationship.

## LETTING GO OF YESTERDAYS

Experiencing this renewal and other possibilities that emerge from embracing the unknown is impossible until we let the past die. We need to let go of yesterday. The record of the past is the foundation upon which we built up a structure of false assumptions. The more we attempt to recapture the past, the more we miss the "new" God is doing now.

In the Bible, God tells us, "For I am about to do something new. See, I have already begun!" (Isa. 43:19 NLT). Part of counting the cost and picking up our cross is trusting God in letting the old die so He can begin a "new." This is what it means to embrace the kind of mystery Jesus talked about of losing your life in order to gain it (see Matt. 16:25).

Embracing mystery and letting go of the old is never a comfortable process. It is ambiguous and uncertain. But this is what prompts us to cling to our faith in God. And this is what demands His intervention.

You may be thinking, *I don't know if I can let go of feeling neglected* or *I'm not sure how to stop thinking about my wife's infidelity* or *Can my husband and I really find peace in the middle of this tumultuous marriage with all we've been through?*

The beauty of a kingdom marriage is that the designer is God Himself. He is the one who is able to renew our marriages by eclipsing the past with new possibilities. Even in the midst of the suffering, pain, and brokenness of a failing marriage, if we submit to God instead of submitting to our selfish, consumer-oriented desires— wanting to be in control, be right, look good, and feel good—He can renew our inner being and ultimately our marriage. This only happens, however, if we reinvent our relationship to the past, which will transform the power it has over us and give Him permission to bring about transformation.

When we allow God to get into the middle of our marriages and submit to His will, He not only transforms our character, but He transforms the value of the very things that caused us harm or were unhealthy in the past. God's intervention in these things creates an opportunity for healing and renewal. Even our failures as spouses can be turned into learning lessons that can bless our marriage and even those around us.

Sure we have to designify our past—the hurts we've been caused, the hurts we've caused—but there is more to transformation than just that. God has the power to take the bad things, even what we consider our character flaws, our lapses in judgment, our bad decisions, and turn them into blessings in disguise. God transforms us by taking those things we judge as bad or evil that we have thought, said, or done, and turning them into strengths or gifts, if we are willing to live in the light. This is what spiritual transformation is all about.

A year or so after counseling Mark and Rene, they shared with my wife and me how God transformed a particular aspect of their marriage that relates exactly to what I'm talking about.

Mark admitted that he finally realized how selfish his need for Rene's attention had been, especially when it came to their sex life. He said they had a breakthrough in this regard because not only had their sex life increased in quality and quantity, but their intimacy in conversation had been dramatically heightened during this time.

Rene nodded in agreement. "When Mark turned that sensitivity from himself on me," she explained, "I was completely overwhelmed by his love and appreciation. He recognized things about me I didn't know anybody could see or appreciate. It transformed the way I view him and I began to experience respect where I formerly experienced contempt."

Mark chimed in. "In the beginning I couldn't take Rene's sharp edge and eye for detail. To me she seemed critical. But as I began to understand her perspective and she made room to investigate her own assumptions, her griping transformed! The 'edge' that I viewed as a threat was really a powerful commitment to integrity and congruity. Instead of hearing her as if her intentions were solely to criticize and knock me down, I started considering what she was seeing. This transformation opened my eyes to other areas that we had been lacking in, like finances and our relationship with our kids. Though our willingness to be so open initially made us uncomfortable and even hurt in some ways, I realized how powerful it is to have a friend who cares for our future more than just living in the status quo. We are truly becoming a family because we can see specific situations we can pray into and discuss that make a real difference in our way of being together!"

Mark and Rene both agreed that this kind of transformation came through their willingness to suffer through being misunderstood, making mistakes, and feeling alone—all the emotions and feelings that are endured when we let go of the past and allow God to step into our suffering and bring light to our darkness. Standing in the middle of challenges like these pays spiritual dividends far beyond what we know is possible.

What's my point? Suffering in a hurting marriage can bring possibility. It can transform your union and yield the passion to bring you closer to your spouse. It can lead us to love as God has ordained it. Here, in the mere shadows of this world, faith hangs on to the possibility that what looks temporally harsh and horrible can be transformed into something that is eternally passionate and life-changing. Faith is the antithesis of the consumer mindset, which says that anything unpleasant should simply be discarded and replaced.

## A NEW BEGINNING

Before Mark and Rene made the turnaround in their marriage, they had gotten to the point where I was mediating their divorce instead of trying to fix their marriage. Two years of hardcore counseling seemed to be worth nothing as I did my best to wisely help divvy up their assets. It was a gut-wrenching process to orchestrate.

When the subject of the custody of their children came up, the mood transformed from bitterness to sadness. Mark and Rene burst out, almost simultaneously, that they didn't want to go through with the divorce. It was a surreal moment. It was as if all the things we discussed came alive in one moment for the two of them. They wanted to give their marriage another chance. They wanted to really listen to each other. They wanted to let go of what they thought they knew about the other person. They wanted to allow God to intervene with His love.

Mark and Rene have now been married for twenty-four years. They are very much in love and are enjoying their renewed, God-designed kingdom marriage. As a matter of fact, they recently shared with me that their romance continues to increase as they maintain their trust in God and embrace mystery while working with the other tools we originally practiced in our sessions. They say no to the temptation of being a consumer spouse. They resist asking, "What's in this for me?" and continue to let go of their addiction to be right and in control. In doing all of these things, they are influencing the kingdom of God in a powerful way.

When will that surreal moment of surrender come for you in your marriage? What will it take for you to realize that God has called you to a mystery not a purchase agreement? That He has invited you into a conversation, not a stump speech to promote your personal agenda? Be encouraged that no matter how bad you think your marriage is right now, there is hope. All is not lost.

If your marriage is not ailing in any way, use these lessons like a businessperson might use *The Wall Street Journal* or *Forbes* magazine to build their foundation, keep an eye on the market, or to get a better grasp on the trends that may be coming up. You can use this book to check, strengthen, or expand the foundations of a kingdom marriage so you are better prepared when tough times do eventually come. Understanding how to live marriage in a way that expresses the kingdom will help you to weather future storms.

# HIGHLIGHTS

- A consumer-oriented marriage teaches us that we are the focal point of our marriage. It's about our needs getting met. It's about us.

- God commissions us to live a kingdom marriage where the relationship is the highest good. We are called to be who we ought to be, even though our spouse may not be who they ought to be.

- The first step to experiencing a renewed and transformational marriage is to look at it and start living it from a kingdom perspective. Otherwise whatever tools you apply will be used to accomplish the purposes of a consumer, not a servant in the kingdom of God.

- Being in a kingdom marriage means submitting to God and your spouse. We are called to give of ourselves in a sacrificial way.

- When we submit in this fashion, we embrace mystery. God is part mystery and so we, created in His image, are part mystery. When we understand that we don't know everything about ourselves, our spouse, or our marriage, we open the possibility to experience our marriage and our spouse in new ways.

- Letting the past go is critical to moving forward into a kingdom marriage, where God is the focal point. He is the one who can bring transformation, even out of our pains and suffering. He is the one who can turn what we thought were curses into blessings.

Chapter Two

# SAY WHAT?

Watch your thoughts; they become words.

Watch your words; they become actions.

Watch your actions; they become habits.

Watch your habits; they become character.

Watch your character; it becomes your destiny.

*Author Unknown*

In the eighties I read an article in a Denver newspaper about a homeless man in Colorado who was found frozen to death in a refrigerated boxcar. At first glance the facts of the case seem obvious and it's pretty clear why he died. Late one night the tired man climbed into a freight car for shelter. The door slid shut and locked before he noticed that it was refrigerated. By the time he read the posting, it was too late. He couldn't get out of the car and froze as a result.

However, when the body was discovered the next morning, it was noted that the refrigeration unit had been broken for many days and the car was awaiting repair. The temperature in the freight car was in the sixties when the door was opened, yet the man's body looked exactly like it would have had he been frozen. The investigators of the case initially remarked that this man died because he *thought* he was going to freeze. What happened? One speculation was that his body took on the characteristics of that assumption.

### WHAT ARE YOU SAYING?

This story stuck with me because I believe it is a powerful metaphor for conversation, the inner dialogue that is running through our heads. Think about it for a minute.

Aren't you always talking to yourself about something? Aren't you always making assumptions or creating stories in your head about what is going on? For instance, if your best friend cancels a lunch with you at the last minute, you might assume she has better plans than hanging out with you. If you didn't get that promotion, you might assume you're really not that smart. If your spouse seems distant and withdrawn, you might assume he is having an affair.

These conversations are very powerful in any relationship, especially in marriage, because they act like static on a radio. They distort and block information in crucial conversations with your spouse, skewing how you view and act within your marriage.

Most of the time we are not even aware of the internal conversation going on in our heads; it's automatic and not something we pay much attention to. But consciously or not, these conversations lock us into habitual behavior and create what we call "ruts," relational conditions that reduce trust, increase frustration and despair, and even plant seeds of contempt for each other.

Conversation can bring both life and death to our marriages. "Death and life are in the power of the tongue, and those who love its use will eat its fruit" (Prov. 18:21 NET). The writer of this passage offers that the location of life and death is the tongue. It is the tool we use to generate fruit in our relationships.

Deuteronomy 30:19 tells us, "Today I invoke heaven and earth as a witness against you that I have set life and death, blessing and curse, before you. Therefore choose life so that you and your descendants may live!" (NET). God sends "heaven" (the spirit realm) and "earth" (the physical realm) to witness against us. The spiritual and the physical are forces that respond to decisions we make and how we act. Therefore in every circumstance we are given the opportunity to choose either life or death through what inner conversations we have.

I know when I allow deadly conversations to dominate me, I make assumptions about my spouse that are generally untrue. These assumptions run wild, and inevitably I find myself being accusatory, defensive, and hostile toward my wife. There is no room to connect with her on any healthy level because these conversations are consuming me.

In these moments I am a lot like the man in that boxcar. I have been locked into a box created by my matrix of automatic assumptions, conversations that seem to be ever present. I am frozen. I cannot call for help to anyone on the outside to open the door. Consequently my marriage is trapped.

If we are willing to answer the challenge of noticing the conversation that occurs automatically for us, then we open the possibility for transforming the kind of person we are being with our spouse. Our willingness to develop the ability to invent and reinforce conversations regardless of what we are going through is what leads us to experiencing a marriage beyond our wildest dreams or a marriage that turns into a nightmare.

## IN THE BEGINNING

Where did the inner conversations we have and the assumptions we form as a result come from? John's gospel begins with an amazing description of God, and I would like to return our attention to Erasmus's translation:

> *It all arose out of a conversation, conversation within God, in fact the conversation was God. So, God started the discussion, and everything came out of this, and nothing happened without consultation.*
>
> *This was the life, life that was the light of men, shining in the darkness, a darkness which neither understood nor quenched its creativity. (John 1:1–14)*

*The conversation was God?* What does this mean? It means that God is a speaking being who converses and dialogues in relationship with us, His creation. In fact the apostle John offers us an invitation to join in this conversation and discover a new way to live, a new way to be!

We live in conversation because we came out of the conversation that God is. Conversation is light. According to 1 John 1:7, "If we walk in the light, as he [God] is in the light, we have fellowship with one another." If you think about it, it makes sense. Conversation is when two or more people talk about what they think and how they feel about a particular topic. How they talk—the words they use, their body posture, the tone of their voice—reveals or sheds light on where they are coming from.

How you love your spouse is determined by what comes out of your mouth. And to some degree, the ability to intentionally convey your inner life to your spouse determines the quality of your married life together.

Perhaps you feel the urge to hide some feelings you need your spouse to see. You love your spouse effectively if you create a conversation to communicate those thoughts instead of shutting down or hiding. Perhaps you feel like blaming your spouse when something doesn't turn out the way they had promised. Rather than attacking them, you can design a conversation to convey the way you were impacted by their actions.

## NOTICING IS THE HARDEST PART

This all starts with the conversations we have with ourselves. We cannot learn how to love out loud if we are boxed into a matrix of deadly self-conversations. We cannot learn to dialogue with our spouse in a healthy manner if we are plagued by assumptions we invent about them or our marriage. We cannot learn how to see our spouse in a new way until we notice what we say to ourselves about who we are "certain" they are or what their intentions are.

Take on this challenge to really hone in on what I'm talking about. For one week, or even a couple of days, journal all the thoughts and conversations that run through your head on a given day. Whatever you are telling yourself about anything, write it down. I bet you will be shocked to see the extent of the inner dialogue that can run rampant in your mind.

## BREAKING THROUGH TO THE TRUTH

What will it take to break through the limiting conversations and assumptions that seem to rule our lives?

In Matthew 11:12–15, Jesus says: "From the days of John the Baptist until now, the kingdom of heaven has been forcefully advancing, and forceful men lay hold of it. For all the Prophets and the Law prophesied until John. And if you are willing to accept it, he is the Elijah who was to come. He who has ears, let him hear." Jesus had a specific audience in mind when He said this. He was talking to those who had a difficult time thinking "out of the box" as it concerned how they viewed God and how and why He does things. He uses the imagery of violence to describe the efforts of moving toward a new and open way of thinking.

The philosopher Martin Heidegger writes about what it takes for us to change our way of being with our spouse, and posits that any such attempt "constantly has the character of doing violence, whether to the claims of the everyday interpretation or to its complacency and its tranquilized obviousness."[1] What is this violence being referred to here? It is the kind of violence one suffers when awakened to a new reality that was hidden in the shadow of assumptions.

It reminds me of Aron Ralston, the hiker who in 2003 was trapped by an eight-hundred-pound boulder and made the choice to amputate his own arm in order to save his life. After five days of being pinned to a Utah canyon wall and finally realizing there was no way out, he had to break free in a literal sense. A move that cost him an arm. It was an unimaginable decision that provoked a violent effort, but it was the only way Aron knew to transform his situation.

Seeing through these shadows begins by asking who God is for us. A. W. Tozer has said,

> *Our idea of God [should] correspond as nearly as possible to the true being of God.... A right conception of God is ... to practical Christian living ... what the foundation is to the temple; where it is inadequate or out of plumb the whole structure must sooner or later collapse. I believe there is scarcely an error in doctrine or a failure in applying Christian ethics that cannot be traced finally to imperfect and ignorant thoughts about God.*[2]

Jesus knew our view of Him mattered. This is why He asked His disciple Peter, "Who do you say I am?" (Matt. 16:15).

**1.** Take a couple of minutes right now and meditate on the question: **Who is God?** What is the conversation you carry on in your head about God that creates how you view Him?

Your response determines what is possible with and through God. It especially governs how we act in relationship with our spouses. For instance, if I believe Jesus is a hard taskmaster and punishing executioner, I will live my life trying to avoid making Him mad. Consequently my relationships will be marked with fear and timidity. I will take great caution to please others at whatever cost, even if it means I am not fully giving my true self or being honest with who I am, what I feel, and how I think.

## HOLDING NOTHING BACK

If I view God as a loving and gracious father who is generous and eagerly desires to be in relationship with His children, I will fully engage life with a deep passion for human interaction and connection. I will be willing to learn from my mistakes for the sake of being in relationship.

This truth lies at the core of the parable of the talents Jesus told.

> *It's ... like a man going off on an extended trip. He called his servants together and delegated responsibilities. To one he gave five thousand dollars, to another two thousand, to a third one thousand, depending on their abilities. Then he left. Right off, the first servant went to work and doubled his master's investment. The second did the same. But the man with the single thousand dug a hole and carefully buried his master's money.*
>
> *After a long absence, the master of those three servants came back and settled up with them. The one given five thousand dollars showed him how he had doubled his investment. His master commended him: "Good work! You did your job well. From now on be my partner."*
>
> *The servant with the two thousand showed how he also had doubled his master's investment. His master commended him: "Good work! You did your job well. From now on be my partner."*

*The servant given one thousand said, "Master, I know
you have high standards and hate careless ways, that
you demand the best and make no allowances for error.
I was afraid I might disappoint you, so I found a good
hiding place and secured your money. Here it is, safe
and sound down to the last cent."*

*The master was furious. "That's a terrible way to live!
It's criminal to live cautiously like that! If you knew I
was after the best, why did you do less than the least?
The least you could have done would have been to
invest the sum with the bankers, where at least I would
have gotten a little interest.*

*"Take the thousand and give it to the one who risked
the most. And get rid of this 'play-it-safe' who won't go
out on a limb. Throw him out into utter darkness."*
*(Matt. 25:14–30 MSG)*

God is not pleased with those who play it safe. This is not
solely because these people are living life being extra careful or pru-
dent, but because they are doing so based on their negative view
of God. They don't use the talents, abilities, and freedom He gives
them because they believe they risk His wrath if things don't work
out as positively as they think they should. They view Him as a
judgmental, unforgiving boss. But this is not who God is.

God is not a sinister being who is waiting for us to screw up.
He is abounding in love and desires to partner with us to further

His kingdom. He wants us to wake up to this truth (see Eph. 5:14). He wants us to shift from simply subsisting in life to exploring the possibilities that arise when we stop limiting Him. This is why it is important to regularly meditate on the question I posed and study the Scriptures to see the true characteristics of God.

## RUINOUS ASSUMPTIONS

In a similar vein we need to ask the same question of our spouse so we can open ourselves up to the opportunities that can bring transformation to our marriage. To really engage in that question, we must start listening to the ongoing, internal conversation we have about them.

The power of these conversations is evidenced in the case of my cousin Len (who also happens to be one of my best friends) and his wife, Sara. As you read through their story, notice the conversations polluting his head and the assumptions he allows to dominate his mind and his emotions. See if you can relate to where he is coming from.

In the winter of 2001, Len was spending a lot of time away from home developing a new office for his financial services business. During these months Sara often told him how much she missed him and how she wished they could set aside some time to do something wonderful together. Though she missed him terribly, Sara told me Len assured her the busy season would soon be over and things would be different.

In the beginning of December, Sara began to leave the house at unusual times. Len would call home looking for Sara and find a babysitter staying with the kids. When he asked Sara where she had been, she said that she had been Christmas shopping, as she often said when she'd been out. Though Len didn't see any presents, he just shrugged off the funny feelings he was starting to have.

Then one day Len called me and wanted to talk. He told me Sara was meeting a friend for lunch at noon. Len explained that a little bit after 12:00, the phone rang and he answered it. On the other end of the phone was the friend Sara was supposed to be meeting for lunch; she was looking for Sara. Len was worried and told her, "I thought she was having lunch with you." There was a long silence from the caller followed by a hurried, "Oh yeah, that's right. I forgot. I better get on my way."

Len was distraught and asked me, "Dan, what would you do?"

"About what?"

Len was quick to reply, "About the call from Sara's friend."

"What are you making up?" I asked. "What are you assuming is going on?"

He thought for a moment. "I'm wondering if she is seeing somebody else." There was a pregnant pause for about ten seconds, then he piped up, "What would you do, Dan?"

"I would let her know my fear and why it has been stirred up."

Len didn't waste much time and said, "If she was having an affair, do you think she would tell me?"

I sighed. On one hand I could understand his frustration, but on the other hand I wasn't a psychic and didn't know exactly what was going on. "Honestly, Len, I'm not sure."

After that call Len's fear turned into outright suspicion. He started waiting for Sara to come home from work and as she got dinner ready, Len searched for the mysterious Christmas presents. He found none. One day Len discovered a card that read "Joe's" along with a phone number written in Sara's handwriting. Getting more and more agitated, he called the number and a man answered. Len asked the stranger his name and the voice on the other end replied, "Joe. Why?" Len hung up quickly, not answering his question and wiping the sweat that was pouring down his face.

My cousin debated with himself whether or not Sara was having an affair with Joe. The thought began as a hunch and gradually infected the way he related to her and their life together. The questions, feelings, and thoughts birthed from Len's suspicion caused his heart and mind to race back and forth, analyzing the past several months.

*We had been communicating so well,* Len thought. Yet he had been away from home a lot working in Europe. Perhaps Sara had become so lonely in his absence she sought out other companionship. Or maybe she found herself being pursued by another man. The thoughts began to pour into Len's mind nonstop. His inner conversations began to boil with contempt and fear, but he did not say a word to Sara. His deadly assumptions were beginning to work their spell on him, and he later confessed to me that he wondered if his marriage was on the rocks.

A few days later as Len and I played a game of golf, he explained the situation to me. I suggested that he take Sara to the movies so that they would have some time alone together. He hastily arranged for somebody to sit with the children and called Sara with his impromptu invitation. To his dismay Sara turned him down flat, saying that she was too tired and had too much to do the next morning. When Len called me, I tried to reassure him that she really may have been tired and suggested that he might want to talk to her to ease his mind. Again, poisonous doubt plagued him and he cut the conversation with me short and hung up. He couldn't stop asking himself, *Has someone else won Sara's heart because I have neglected her?*

One day I suggested that he and Sara have dinner with Aileen and me at our home. Len and I made official plans and picked the date. He decided that on their way home after dinner he would finally confront Sara about his growing suspicions.

Len called me the morning of our dinner date. This time he was more distraught than I had heard him up until that time. He was considering canceling his next trip to Europe, anticipating he would have too much work to do on his relationship with Sara. When I asked why he was so desperate, he said, "Sara called me from work. She asked if she could meet me at your house because she had errands to run before dinner." Visions of a pre-dinner rendezvous with some guy name Joe grabbed Len by the throat. I noticed he had become very rigid in his speech, convinced she was deeply involved with Joe. I convinced Len to wait until after our dinner that evening to make any drastic decisions. At least then he would have had the benefit of talking to Sara about what was going on.

For the rest of the day Len called me numerous times obsessing about all the "evidence." He was so upset that I offered to pick him up and drive him to my house. He was incredibly moody, worried, and sullen the entire car ride. We stopped at a grocery store and, while I was inside, Len unsuccessfully attempted to relax. It was impossible. All he could think about were the hours that lay ahead and what might happen … perhaps a confession of infidelity … perhaps the beginning of the end of their marriage.

As we drove to my house, Len sarcastically blurted out, "Great. This is going to be one terrific night. Sara is probably going to be late coming from who knows where and I can't think about anything other than uncovering the affair." I just stared at him and shook my head. As we pulled up the driveway, it was obvious he was dreading seeing his wife. What would he say? What if his worst fears were true? His heart was so heavy that I was sure it was going to break when he saw her.

When we walked into the house, we heard a thunderous "SURPRISE! HAPPY BIRTHDAY!" You can only imagine Len's shock; before him stood fifty of his closest friends—many of whom he hadn't seen in years—laughing, smiling, and taking pictures. Standing next to a magnificent birthday cake was Sara with tears in her eyes and a big smile on her face.

Tears streamed down his own face as Len embraced his lovely wife. "You don't know how surprised I am," he managed to whisper. As he admired the cake, he asked her if she had made it. "No," Sara replied. "I bought it at Joe's." Her words turned his subjective fear to ashes. Everything that had seemed so real to him moments before vanished into emptiness.

Len's assumptions were unfounded and untrue. The tremendous anxiety he felt as a result of his inner conversations was for naught. He had created a reality that didn't even exist, and so he was unable to explore what other possibilities could have explained the evidence.

## LIVING IN THE MATRIX

"What is real? How do you define real?" These were the questions posed by Morpheus to Neo in the movie *The Matrix*. The movie opens with Neo being contacted by Morpheus through a computer message. The message reads, "Do you want to know what the Matrix is, Neo?" Soon after this, Morpheus makes physical contact with Neo and begins to reveal the shocking truth about the Matrix. To his absolute amazement Neo discovers that what he thought was real was nothing more than a computer-generated simulation intended to give human beings the illusion of freedom.

Do we live in a matrix? Is what we think of as reality, really real? Len was convinced that Sara was having an affair. For him, it was as real as the book you are holding in your hand. He acted from that interpretation, and it caused him to imagine his wife betraying him. The resulting damaging effects had him acting accordingly—fearful, suspicious, and angry. But in reality there was no reason for him to feel the things he was feeling. After all, Sara was simply planning a surprise birthday party for him.

Think about your own marriage. Do things like this happen often for you? Do you create realities in your mind that are not real? Do you ever imagine something happening only to find out that it isn't true? Do you make assumptions about your spouse based on bits and pieces of information, not the whole story? I'm sure it's a challenge for many of us.

Making assumptions about our spouse keeps us boxed into a matrix of predictable and predetermined reactions toward them that are congruent with the matrix of conversations we have in our head about what we think is going on. The matrix robs us of our ability to freely draw on our creative power to love our spouse the way we would want them to love us.

I am afraid of what might have happened that evening between Len and Sara if he had not been surprised by her extreme act of generosity. He was so locked into the matrix of suspicion that I shudder to think of what he may have said or done in that hurtful state.

### I NEVER THOUGHT OF THAT BEFORE

The question for us all is, how can we begin to take notice of these conversations that we have ignored all along? It's clear to us that while Len was having his inner conversations about Sara betraying him, he was unaware of the power of those thoughts. That unexamined assumption was like a chemical, poisoning his attitude toward Sara.

During the party I asked Len what was going on with him in the car on the way over to my house. I knew he had been troubled, but I wanted to explore it further. In talking with me, Len realized that while he was worried and upset, it never occurred to him that he was suspicious.

Had he investigated this particular feeling and looked at the situation from different angles, Len would have been able to maintain a much healthier perspective about his wife and their marriage. When I asked him why he didn't just ask his wife about the name he found on the paper, he said, "I didn't believe she would tell me the truth."

I replied, "That is the suspicion I was referring to. Do you see how it kept you locked in a box and prevented you from considering any other possibilities?"

What could Len have done? He could have asked himself if it was really true that his wife was having an affair based on the sole evidence of a piece of paper with the name "Joe" on it. He could have thought about what else could be true. Perhaps it was a reminder to call the plumber. Perhaps it was a name of a guest she saw on *Oprah*. Instead he allowed his conversation to trap him.

As we explored Len's situation, I reminded him of an argument that he and Sara had years ago that Aileen and I overheard while in their home. They had been discussing a bill that hadn't been paid and it exploded into quite a drama. This all happened while the four of us were having a glass of wine in the kitchen just before our plans to see a movie.

"No, Len, I am not going to work because we need money!" is what Len heard his wife say.

He became furious. "Listen, Sara, if we are going to be able to make it financially, I need support with the bills! Now that we have a child, our bills have grown and I can't see how we can do this on my single salary. You need to get a job!"

Sara did not back down. "I know we need more money, but getting a job outside the home will not work for raising Mark [their son] the way we have been discussing since I was pregnant. We've talked about how important it is that I stay home and raise him. I am unwilling to break that boundary and you aren't going to bully me into it!"

With these forceful words Len stormed out of the house and slammed the door. Sitting in the kitchen, Aileen and I were now privy to an awkward situation. Aileen went into the bedroom to talk with Sara. I waited for Len, believing he would eventually return. Fifteen minutes later he did. He decided to take a walk with me to talk a bit.

Len opened up, saying, "You know, Dan, I don't think I can do this anymore. Sara just doesn't listen. I don't think we can make it.

All we do is fight about money. Sometimes I feel like she is taking advantage of me!"

I looked Len in the eyes and asked him, "Do you remember that store you opened in Southern California?" When Len was twenty-four years old, he had taken the money he saved during college and negotiated a lease on a restaurant in La Jolla, California, which is where he met Sara.

My question caught him by surprise and he answered in a drawn-out and suspicious tone, "Yeeeah?"

I continued. "You did the same thing in that situation that you are doing now. You came to me after a year there and said, 'Dan, will you help me negotiate my way out of this disaster? It just isn't workable. The people here don't like this location. They prefer the other side of town and it seems impossible to draw them into the restaurant!' Remember how you wanted to get out?"

He responded even more uncertainly, "Uh-huh?"

"Len, after looking at the books and analyzing the market, I told you I thought the restaurant could do well, that the problem wasn't the location but the operator—you. I think I said something to the effect that you leaving and doing something else was like rearranging the deck furniture on the *Titanic*. You even acknowledged then that if you didn't face what needed to change in you, you would still have to face yourself one day if you were ever to really be happy. Well, Len, honestly, I believe this is that time, because it seems to me that you are engaging the same strategy with Sara right now that you engaged in La Jolla." (Len sold the restaurant at a discounted price, thinking it had no chance of making it in that location. Today, twenty-three years later, the family who bought it from him is still running that business and has since opened three other restaurants in the surrounding area.)

"You and Sara have some differences. You are probably right that she may not listen to you as well as she should. Still, I haven't heard you tell me anything about how you have contributed to the situation you and Sara now find yourselves in. For instance, when she says it's difficult for her to hear you or vice versa, I wonder how you have been relating to her. Because you haven't bothered to think about that, I find it hard to believe that you have really done everything you can to come to terms with her."

In both cases Len's default conversation had trapped him. He indulged in conversations that revolved around blaming his circumstances and attacking others for the way things turned out. By continuing to engage in such deadly inner dialogue, he missed out on the opportunity to explore his contribution to the situations. By blaming circumstances and attacking Sara, Len rendered himself helpless. In one instance Len blamed the store's failure on the location; in the other instance he blamed and attacked Sara for being the reason they couldn't talk about their financial dilemma.

I heard how Len had lost his temper with Sara. Being curious about Sara wasn't even in his thinking because he thought he knew her and didn't need to notice his own conversation. Len was too busy assuming to stop and challenge his thoughts and ask Sara for hers. I reminded him that Sara never said she wasn't willing to work. She was saying she wanted her son to have a stable home life.

Len reacted immediately. "Well, doesn't that mean she doesn't want to help me with the finances?"

I waited a moment to think about how to respond and then replied, "Well, I guess it *could* mean that, but I wonder what could be as true as that, or even more likely?"

My cousin thought for about a minute and posed the question back to me. "Dan, can *you* think of what could be as true as what I have said or even more likely?"

"Yes." The answer jumped from my lips like it had its own life. "Maybe she has been thinking of ways to support the family from home as she raises Mark. Or maybe she is willing to consider such a possibility with your support."

"I never thought of that before. I wonder why?" Len responded.

I took the opportunity to posit a possibility. "Maybe because up until now, those prospects did not fit the box life comes in for you. Can you see how you have tried to fit Sara and your marriage into a box that makes you right and gives you a sense of control and predictability?" We spoke for a bit more about how Len's inability to recognize and question his assumptions was one of the indicators of how trapped in his box he was. As Len quietly listened, I could tell he was processing.

We got back to the house and he immediately went to find Sara to ask for forgiveness. He realized how he boxed her in with his assumptions, and wanted to start working on other options with her. That day, Len and Sara had the first of many breakthrough conversations that led to Sara starting a very successful day-care business. Later she opened her own consulting firm for people who were interested in getting into that field of work. Eventually Sara became the ombudsman for day-care services in the county where she lived.

## NEW POSSIBILITIES

Len was completely boxed in by the conversations that were running him. By exploring his own conversations about Sara and asking for her to help, a new possibility emerged that otherwise would have gone ignored. That conversation was the beginning of a new way for Len to relate to Sara.

Len later told me that up until that time, Sara was an obstacle in getting his way. He never saw her as a partner. In fact he told me that when he started to relate to her that way he couldn't believe how much of her beauty and wisdom he had been missing out on.

The freedom that comes from reaching outside of the matrix of our automatic conversations creates new and unprecedented possibilities for us to be together in marriage. We will experience new things, good things that have never happened before. Think about this. The apostle Paul wrote in 2 Corinthians 5:17 (KJV), "Therefore if any man be in Christ, he is a new creature: old things are passed away; behold, all things are become new." *New* means something that has never been before. Transformation in our marriages will always result in something new even if it is an old challenge.

To get a sense of what legacy Len was creating in his marriage, we explored what kind of future would open up if he continued to indulge his suspicious conversations that caused him to blame and attack his wife. I asked him to look up the definition of the word *suspicion* and to imagine the environment it generates as a conversation.

Len read, "The imagination of the existence of something

without proof, or upon very slight evidence, or upon no evidence at all. Suspicion often proceeds from the apprehension of evil; it is the offspring or companion of jealousy. *Nature itself, after it has done an injury, will ever be suspicious, and no man can love the person he suspects* (South)."[3]

I offered to Len the truth that when we indulge our automatic tendencies to suspect others, we are actually suspecting God. Therefore we can't love others or God. We condemn ourselves to a life of loneliness and resentment that will result in isolation. It hinders and sometimes even prohibits our ability to connect with people and drives others away.

When he started challenging his inner conversations, Len finally woke up and he literally invented new ways of being with Sara. He shared some of his thoughts with me in a letter I had asked him to write about how he loved her out loud by challenging his own conversations.

> *I have experienced profound breakthroughs in intimacy and compassion for Sara by letting her know how I feel when we are talking. I have always had a difficult time communicating my emotions, so I started to do what you suggested when I start getting angry or resentful and wanting to attack or blame. I let Sara know what I am feeling in my body. Usually my throat tightens and I get a dry mouth and then I want to get away from her, which I do by either walking out on her or attacking her to get her to leave. Just talking about those symptoms has*

*opened a whole world of emotional intimacy for me and most of all Sara. She says she really feels loved when I include her this way.*

*Surprisingly most of these conversations end up very tender and compassionate. A number of times she has been able to weep in my arms and tell me how alienated from me she has felt in the past and how despairing our marriage had become for her. My compassion for her has been overwhelming a couple of times. We never dreamed we could have such intimacy and trust with each other. The irony for me is that I always thought if I talked about these things out loud it would destroy our lives together. I am learning that what makes the difference is not that we talk, but how we talk. This revelation is revolutionizing our marriage! As you say, Dan, it is a life together that for us is unprecedented. We have never been this way before!*

Once Len realized the conversations in his head were a background story that had influenced the destiny he had been living out in his marriage, he took the challenge to interrupt those thoughts. With God's grace Len and Sara are now rewriting their destiny one conversation at a time.

Consider that we can choose how we view others or how we relate to them through our inner conversation about them. As soon as we notice our default conversation, we can stop it and create a new way of talking to ourselves about others and the situations we find ourselves in.

## STOP AND LISTEN

Take a moment and notice the inner conversations you are having while reading this book. Are you really investigating the possibilities that can be available to you and your spouse through what I am writing? Or are you already disproving or searching for exceptions to what you have read before spending any time at all exploring it?

Are you having life-giving conversations like "I'm excited to put these truths into practice" or "I can see how my assumptions have infected my relationship"? Are you having deadly conversations like "This book is a waste of time" or "I've done this before and it hasn't worked"?

What if, instead of accepting each and every thought that comes into your mind about God, your spouse, or your marriage, you stop and think about it? By questioning the reality of your conversation, you open up the possibility of renewing your marriage in ways you would never have imagined. You experience a freedom that relieves you of unnecessary anxiety and helps to maintain a healthy perspective about your spouse and the future of your marriage. As Søren Kierkegaard said, it takes "great courage to dare to look at yourself." Noticing our conversations can be quite a challenge.

Here is a practical exercise that will help you see the deadly conversations you have that affect your relationship with your spouse. This is a great tool to use when these conversations actually come up. You can become more aware of the assumptions running through your head and engage in discussions in a healthy and life-giving way.

**2.** Think of a topic of conversation that you have had or often have with your spouse that results in an argument. It's the one you dread having because of how heated you both get and how impossible a resolution seems.

**3.** Write down what you assume you know your spouse will say or do that so irritates you. What are you so certain they will say in response to your opinions or thoughts? How do you assume they will react? What do you assume about where they are coming from?

**4.** As you write and read through the assumptions you make about your partner or your marriage in these conversations, notice how you feel on a physical and emotional level. Do you tense up? Do you start shaking? Write down what your body experiences. Now notice your emotions. Are you frustrated? Angry? Peeved? Write down every emotion you experience.

**5.** After you have recognized your feelings resulting from your assumptions, ask yourself what you are assuming about your spouse in that situation. For example, do you assume your wife is selfish because she won't allow you to get another job? Do you assume your husband is abandoning you because he works all the time? What assumptions have you made about your spouse that keep you from exploring this topic of conversation further?

**6.** Now think about some other possibilities that could be as true or even more likely than what you initially assumed. Meditate on the possibilities that could be present if you stop believing the conversation you have in your head and instead challenge the assumptions you make. What do you believe can open up in your marriage?

Perhaps your relationship with your spouse is frozen in certain areas right now because of automatic conversations that you never noticed before. Maybe you did realize the assumptions you were making, but you rationalized them to such an extent they are now harmful influences in your way of relating to your spouse.

Imagine the new possibilities that might open up out of answering the challenge of just noticing your own automatic conversation. Imagine the transformation. Imagine the romance. Imagine a new way of being together. Imagine the destiny. What you are imagining can only be found when you break free from the matrix of default conversation and enter into the possibility of an unprecedented life together.

Where do you start living this marriage beyond your wildest dreams?

One of the best places to start developing the unprecedented is to learn what it is like to truly love your spouse. This is where the consumer and kingdom concepts begin to clash before our eyes. This is where we realize the skins of consumerism we need to shed in order to shut down the voices in our head that demand the things we think we need. This is where we must learn about our "other."

## HIGHLIGHTS

- We are always engaged in conversations in our heads that can bring either life or death in our marriage.

- What we believe about who God is, is crucial to noticing who we believe our spouse is.

- If we are not aware of our inner dialogue, we can create realities that simply do not exist and that can be deadly to our marriage.

- When we start to notice what we are saying about our spouse and our marriage, we can be open to new possibilities that can revitalize our marriage.

## Chapter Three

# BUT WHAT ABOUT ME?

Hardly anything else reveals so well the fear
and uncertainty among men as the length to
which they will go to hide their true selves
from each other and even from their own
eyes.... The result of this lifelong dissimulation
is that people rarely know their neighbors
for what they really are, and worse than
that, the camouflage is so successful that
they do not know themselves either.

*A. W. Tozer* [1]

When we act as a consumer in our marriages, we feel a sense of entitlement to look good, feel good, be right, and be in control. We position ourselves in our relationship to get what we want. And if things don't turn out the way we feel they should, we want to make our spouse pay until it does. Until our demands are met, we will not be who we said we would be when we said our marriage vows.

Time after time I hear people say things like this:

"He doesn't make me feel sexy."

"I don't feel appreciated."

"She never listens to me."

"He's always spending his free time with his buddies."

"What will our friends think?"

These statements are clear signs of entitlement. When we are aware of and begin to question those self-seeking desires, we can begin to free ourselves from fear and selfishness. The possibility of truly loving our spouse, or what I like to call "othering," emerges.

I borrow the term "othering" from Old Testament scholar Walter Brueggemann, who writes, "I take the liberty of using the word 'other' as a verb, for I mean to suggest that 'other' is not simply a counter-object, but it is the risky, demanding, dynamic process of relating to one who is not us...."[2]

Dr. Brueggemann is speaking of the manner in which we relate to God, but this term aptly applies to how we relate to all others, particularly our spouse. Othering is simply loving your spouse by willing their good. While the consumer society tells us that we can only learn to love others if we love ourselves first, othering suggests that we love ourselves best when we love the other first. This is a principle that guides a kingdom marriage.

The challenge of othering lies in the possibility of suffering. Willing the good of our spouse often puts us in a vulnerable place because they are free to hurt us as much as they are free to love us. Our spouse is free to use us, abandon us, manipulate us, betray us, lie to us, and so on. It's awful to even think about. After all, none of us want to be used, abandoned, manipulated, betrayed, or lied to.

So what do most of us do? We instinctively want to protect our-selves from the risks of being in relationship with the other. We want to keep our marriage about ourselves as much as we can. It's the only way we can survive and make sure our spouse doesn't rob us of what we feel we are entitled to.

There are three basic strategies we employ to do this. We hide, we blame, and we attack.

**Hide**. Adam and Eve did this in the garden after they disobeyed God and ate the forbidden fruit. Hiding is another form of cover-ing up. Feeling ashamed, Adam and Eve covered up their nakedness with leaves. We hide what we think others will judge and use for themselves. For instance, if we did something wrong that may put our spouse's view of us at stake, we cover up the mistake.

**Blame**. We blame God and others much like Adam did when he told God, "It's Your fault I sinned. You are the one who gave me the woman who caused me to stumble." We place the reasons for our failures on God, our spouse, or our circumstances. We can even blame ourselves and hide in our guilt so we don't have to face the pain we may have caused others.

**Attack**. We attack our spouse much like Satan attacked God when he accused God of being a liar by withholding the Tree of Knowledge of Good and Evil from Adam and Eve. I'm sure you've heard the saying, "The best offense is a great defense." By launching an all-out assault on our spouse's character with such generalizations as "you always" and "you never," we think we can distract or keep them from taking whatever we feel entitled to. We can attack through sarcasm, name-calling, and threatening violence.

C. S. Lewis captures this reality in his book *The Four Loves.*

*To love at all is to be vulnerable. Love anything and your heart will certainly be wrung and possibly be broken. If you want to make sure of keeping it intact, you must give your heart to no one, not even an animal. Wrap it carefully round with hobbies and little luxuries; avoid all entanglements; lock it up safe in the casket or coffin of your selfishness. But in that casket—safe, dark, motionless, airless—it will change. It will not be broken; it will become unbreakable, impenetrable, irredeemable. The alternative to tragedy … is damnation. The only place outside of Heaven where you can be perfectly safe from all the dangers and perturbations of love is Hell. I believe that the most lawless and inordinate loves are less contrary to God's will than a self-invited and self-protective lovelessness.[3]*

To other is to be vulnerable and to be honest with ourselves and our spouse about who we are and what lies underneath the facade of our defenses. Just as Jesus said the truth would set us free, exposing the truth of ourselves and our needs brings us a step closer to the freedom of experiencing a transformational marriage.

## WHERE THE BATTLE BEGINS

Karl and Millie met while they were both students at the University of the Nations on the Island of Hawaii. It was a magical time in their lives. They were young and on fire for God and His people. Both had dedicated the next couple of years to Youth with a Mission (YWAM), a missionary organization with bases around the world.

At one point they had spent a year apart in different parts of the globe. Karl had been stationed in northern Italy, and Millie was in Jakarta. While they were separated, they managed to keep their romance alive by promising each other they would one day travel the world together. Karl and Millie wanted to return to the places they had ministered so they could share the experience of the culture with the other. When I began meeting with them, twelve years had passed since they left the mission field and, two kids later, they had never fulfilled that promise.

Karl was working as a vice president for a Fortune 500 company and Millie was a stay-at-home mother and also helped Karl with administrative work in their home office. The couple had adapted well to this lifestyle and was powerfully aligned on how they wanted to raise the kids. They also had in place a well-calculated and profitable financial strategy for the family. In many ways life was turning out the way they had planned when they hired me as their coach.

This couple impressed me. Each time we met I could tell Karl and Millie actually practiced what we worked on between sessions. However, some destructive habits continued to plague their ability to be intimate and threatened their marriage.

New possibility began to emerge between the two of them when Millie started getting honest with herself. She complained that Karl worked way too many hours, and she believed he was obsessed with his work. When he came home, he didn't have much to give to her or the family. Karl's resource of time and energy was slowly getting depleted. Millie told me, "He seems to be less and less available to our kids, who are only seven and nine."

As a dedicated mother and having served two years as a missionary, Millie understood what it means to have a passion for one's work. But she confessed she longed to spend more time with Karl. She felt they were drifting apart because of his obsession with succeeding at work.

Karl also put in his two cents. He felt like Millie constantly put him down and didn't appreciate his hard work and dedication. He felt unappreciated because Millie could not understand how consuming some of his work problems could be. The combination of working on major business negotiations and the complexities of inside politics made his job very difficult. He told me, "I just need some room to unwind a bit and get myself on the same wavelength as the kids and Millie." He also felt like Millie was using her sexuality to manipulate him. Karl once said, "She just doesn't like sex! What am I supposed to do? At least when I am working I feel fulfilled and appreciated."

Do these complaints sound familiar? Listening in on their conversation, we begin to see quickly how they attack each other to protect their own interests.

Looking at me squarely, Millie began. "Dan, I can't talk to Karl about anything but our checking account and the kids' activities. Every time we start to discuss our challenges, he gets angry, shuts down, or leaves the room." Then she turned to her husband, "Karl, you've been working so much that when you come home you are emotionally drained from your work. You are so tired that you aren't really present with me or the kids for the short time we are together at night. And then when we go to bed, there are times when you spend another hour or two working some more."

"Honey, you know how important my work is to me. Why can't you support me in difficult times like this?" Karl retorted, clearly flustered at the accusation.

Millie's response was quick. "I do. I just don't want to continue this disconnect. I think it's bad for the kids and bad for our relationship."

"I hear your frustration."

"Do you think you could plan your life with me so that we don't lose each other? Especially when things get busy? That way you would feel supported along the way and we could keep our relationship alive instead of putting it on hold all the time because you aren't present."

"I do get lost in my thoughts from time to time and lose track of what's going on around me," Karl said, resigned.

"And abandon me and the kids …"

Stung, Karl's reply came with intensity. "Hey, I didn't say that. You did!"

"Well, what would you call it?"

"Millie, can't you just listen to me for a moment before accusing me? I don't want this conversation to degenerate into a cold war or some kind of battle. I feel worthless when you talk to me that way. The truth is, I am drained. I feel like there isn't enough of me to go around. All you do is rob me of my life! You're like a black hole!"

"I thought I was your wife, your partner, you know, your soul mate. Whatever happened to that part of our life together?" Millie dabbed at her eyes with a tissue as the tears came.

"Millie, are you serious? What is that supposed to mean? It isn't like you have been my soul mate either. When was the last time we made love? I feel like you live by a double standard. You want me to be your husband, but you don't want to be a wife! Whatever happened to submitting?"

"What are you talking about? When you say things like that, I feel like all I am to you is a commodity. Jesus never forces the church to submit. It is done out of reverence and love. You aren't listening to me, Karl. All you seem to do is think of yourself when we talk about this subject. I am going to take a breather and stop this before we say things that will hurt each other more than we have already!"

And with that Millie stormed out of the room, slammed the door behind her, and went for a short walk to regain her composure. The irony in this situation is obvious: Millie said she can't talk with Karl because he typically gets angry, shuts down, and leaves the room. Just minutes after saying that, she did the very thing she blamed him for.

## THE VIEW FROM HERE

Outbursts like Millie's tell us about our relational or spiritual life more than we probably care to admit. We don't like hearing what comes out of our mouths when we get caught off guard because, heaven forbid, it certainly can't be what we are really feeling or thinking. Or can it?

In his book *Choice Therapy*, William Glasser talks about how our view of ourselves fluctuates from flattery to pure fantasy. He offers that because we tend to view ourselves through rose-colored glasses, we ignore things that might challenge our inflated self-images. Things that would ultimately help us connect with others.

C. S. Lewis put it this way:

> Surely what a man does when he is taken off his guard
> is the best evidence for what sort of a man he is? Surely
> what pops out before the man has time to put on a
> disguise is the truth? If there are rats in a cellar you are
> most likely to see them if you go in very suddenly. But
> the suddenness does not create the rats: it only prevents
> them from hiding.[4]

Consider C. S. Lewis's quote in light of the conversation Karl and Millie had in my office that day. Their automatic reactions exposed some of their rats. The biggest rat was how entitled they felt in their "positions" as wife and husband. When Karl or Millie wanted to talk about something that was bothering them, the other felt their need to look good, be right, be in control, or feel good was threatened. Both of them imposed self-protective strategies and abandoned the other by hiding behind judgments, blaming the other for what they did or didn't do, and attacking the other's character.

What if the times that we are caught in such vulnerable positions provide a clear view into what is plaguing our marriage? What if it can offer a space for God to break through to open up new possibilities for our marriage? What if these "rats" can truly lead us to transformation?

**1.** Think about the things you feel entitled to that make you look good, feel good, be right, and be in control. Maybe you feel entitled to spending quality time with your husband. Maybe you feel entitled to having sex five times a week with your wife. Write these things down in your journal.

**2.** Now think about the different strategies you use when you feel you are not getting the things you just wrote down. Do you attack your wife and call her names? Do you withdraw from your husband and give him the silent treatment? Write those down.

If you are aware of these actions, you can begin to exercise your freedom and interrupt them before they have an opportunity to infect your conversations with your spouse.

Perhaps the most important thing to begin doing is to say no to our selfish desires and demands. These things seek to control our spouse and so suffocate and ultimately suck the life out of our marriage. The key to othering is to get to a place where we start wanting to do things that transform our marriage—even if it means sacrificing our needs in the moment, and even if it means bringing ourselves temporary suffering.

## MY WILL OR THY WILL?

The main obstacle to othering is our flesh, or our sinful nature. Peter describes how "fleshly lusts … war against the soul" (1 Peter 2:11 KJV). Paul talks about this waging of war in Romans.

> *And I know that nothing good lives in me, that is, in my sinful nature. I want to do what is right, but I can't. I want to do what is good, but I don't. I don't want to do what is wrong, but I do it anyway. But if*

*I do what I don't want to do, I am not really the one doing wrong; it is sin living in me that does it. (Rom. 7:18–20 NLT)*

The word *sin* in this context is an archery term that means "to miss the mark." If you look up the word *character*, you'll find that "mark" is a key definition. *The American Dictionary of the English Language* (1828) defines *character* as "to distinguish by particular marks or traits ... generosity is often a characteristic virtue of a brave man."

Character is the "mark" we leave on people after being with them. It is what they remember about us. When Paul speaks about us missing the mark, he is referring to the character of Christ that is marked by love and generosity toward God and others, or othering. The conflict is that we want to be like Christ—we want to be giving, loving, and respecting spouses—but our flesh gets in the way. Instead of being giving, we have a tendency to take. Instead of being loving, we have a tendency to be ambivalent. Instead of being respectful, we have a tendency to dishonor.

There is a palpable tension between our spirit and our flesh. Appealing to our flesh, or being driven by our impulses, is immediately self-gratifying. We get what we want right away. Appealing to our spirit, or having the same character as Jesus, is a long-term gain. We make sacrifices today for a more meaningful tomorrow.

Dallas Willard writes about the battle between those two forces:

*The human will or "spirit" ... is very different than the flesh actuated in unrestrained desire. It considers alternatives. That is its essential nature. It is our God-given ability by which we have an interest, not just in this [what is immediate], but in what is better or best. It takes a broad view of possibilities; not just of one desire and its object, but of other desires and goods. That is where choice comes in. Choice involves deliberation between alternatives, with a view to what is best. It seeks light. It treasures the law. The conflict between "the flesh" and the [human] spirit is the conflict between desire … and love, which is always directed toward what is good for its objects.*[5]

When the flesh is focused on its desires, we only see others as a way to fulfill our needs. We view them only in the light of how they can be used to meet our needs to look good, feel good, be right, and be in control. When the wheels of our spirits are turning, we have aligned our intentions with God's and are putting our spouse ahead of our consumer demands.

Now we cannot take dominion of that which we do not recognize. By recognizing how and where we are feeding the impulses of our flesh, we can consciously exercise our human spirit by following Jesus' example and truly loving the other.

Take Millie for instance. She gave in to her fleshly impulses when she insinuated that Karl's intention was to "abandon her and the kids." Both the tone she used and what she said are accusatory, not loving. When we get in similar situations, we need to be aware of what we are saying and ask, "Is this how I would want to be loved or talked to?" When we look beyond our demands to our intentions and motivations behind them, we open new and powerful ways to other.

## OTHERING DISCIPLINES

Prayer, meditation, and worship are powerful spiritual disciplines to master the flesh and draw near to God and His purposes in our marriage. Prayer gives us an opportunity to connect with God and allow Him to move in our lives. Meditation offers a space for reflection where we can be open to His promptings. Worship is an opportunity to increase our faith in God's deliverance, His abundance, and love for us and our spouse. Praise develops a grateful heart for His faithfulness to deliver life in any situation that may arise. However, like all tools, these disciplines require more than going through the motions.

Jesus said,

> *Do not judge, or you too will be judged. For in the same way you judge others, you will be judged, and with the measure you use, it will be measured to you. Why do you look at the speck of sawdust in your brother's eye and pay no attention to the plank in your own eye? How can you say to your brother, "Let me take the speck out of your eye," when all the time there is a plank in your own eye? You hypocrite, first take the plank out of your own eye, and then you will see clearly to remove the speck from your brother's eye. (Matt. 7:1–5)*

Jesus is pointing to how we relate to others in the practice of our spiritual disciplines. He requires a contrite heart to be able to connect with the kingdom. This calls for a willingness to be open to God's probing Spirit. In the context of this scripture, we are to self-reflect instead of cast judgment on someone else for what we think they are doing wrong. In the case of marriage, we can ask God for His leading to expose the fleshly ways we relate to our spouse. We can ask Him to open our spiritual eyes. We can ask Him for guidance. We can ask Him for wisdom. All these things can cause us to be more active in submitting our flesh to our spirit.

### Listening Generously

We must be spiritually developed to the point that we are ready to, or that we would rather, do things for a greater good. This only happens when we daily crucify our flesh and live in the Spirit of God. Crucifying our flesh begins with listening generously. When we listen generously, we suspend our need to be heard, understood, and feel wanted or loved so that we can acknowledge and seek to understand what our spouse is saying.

Dr. Brueggemann writes about learning the difference between complaint and praise.

> It is a tricky thing to know when in the presence of God
> to sound self-asserting complaint and when to offer self-
> yielding praise ... with the neighbor it is right to assert
> one's freedom [to complain], and it is right to yield one's
> freedom [to listen] for the neighbor. The demanding
> work is to know when to do what and that requires the
> thoughtful, disciplined practice of negotiation.[6]

Professor Bruce Patton of Harvard University once defined negotiation as "any communication designed to persuade or influence another person to do or not do something." The major way we negotiate in marriage is through complaining. When we tell our spouse that we are unhappy—because we don't feel needed, we feel abandoned, we're not getting quality time with them, we feel unappreciated, and so on—we are trying to persuade them, or negotiate with them, so they recognize our yearning to meet a desire we have.

When we listen to our spouse generously, we are communicating that they are worth listening to. What they have to say matters to us. We become willing to suspend our agendas to connect with them. When people experience this, they are influenced to open up, be vulnerable, and be understanding. Two things embody this practice and both require the exercising of our spirit.

First, we need to hear the content of our spouse's complaint. This is important especially when we feel like interrupting because we believe we are being misunderstood, indicted, cheated, lied to, and so on.

Second, we explore what our spouse is yearning for that is driving their complaint. To yearn is "to feel an earnest desire; that is to have a desire or inclination stretching towards an object or end."[7] When we yearn for something in our marriages, we desire to have it so much that everything in us—our intent, speech, and posture—complains about it.

If there is no yearning, there would be no complaint. We would just settle for what we have because of a lack of a vision for anything beyond our current state. As it concerns marriage, it's important to understand that though you may not be able to meet the particular complaint, understanding the yearning of your spouse brings unity.

Complaining has been a way humans have communicated our longings to God and one another since the beginning of time. Why do we turn to God most of the time? I believe it is because we know He will listen to us and He is generous. In Job, we are told, "You'll pray to [God] and he'll listen; he'll help you do what you've promised" (Job 22:27 MSG). On the contrary, human beings tend to be threatened by or indifferent to our complaining, depending on how it serves their personal agenda. Being a generous listener is not part of our innate nature.

The psalms provide a rich background of experiences for us to draw from in grasping the benefit of understanding the content of complaint and the yearning behind it. These Scriptures speak distinctly and powerfully about how those who have turned to God in their complaints have been delivered, preserved, and saved even from death. Consider these words from Psalm 102:

> *Lord, hear my prayer! Listen to my plea!*
> *Don't turn away from me in my time of distress.*
> *Bend down to listen, and answer me quickly when I*
> *    call to you.*
> *For my days disappear like smoke, and my bones burn*
> *    like red-hot coals.*
> *My heart is sick, withered like grass, and I have lost*
> *    my appetite.*
> *Because of my groaning, I am reduced to skin and*
> *    bones.*

> *I am like an owl in the desert, like a little owl in a*
>    *far-off wilderness.*
> *I lie awake, lonely as a solitary bird on the roof.*
> *My enemies taunt me day after day. They mock and*
>    *curse me.*
> *I eat ashes for food. My tears run down into my drink*
> *because of your anger and wrath.*
> *For you have picked me up and thrown me out.*
> *My life passes as swiftly as the evening shadows.*
> *I am withering away like grass. (Ps. 102:1–11 NLT)*

What are some of the psalmist's complaints?

- *"For my days disappear like smoke, and my bones burn like red-hot coals."* He complains of his short life and his aches and pains in these times of persecution.
- *"My heart is sick, withered like grass, and I have lost my appetite."* He complains of his despair and how he has lost his desire to enjoy a meal or even to nourish his body.
- *"Because of my groaning, I am reduced to skin and bones. I am like an owl in the desert, like a little owl in a far-off wilderness. I lie awake, lonely as a solitary bird on the roof."* He complains of how alienated, lonely, depressed, and misunderstood he feels.

You get the picture. So what are the writer's yearnings? When he complains about how short his life is and how tired he feels, he yearns for more time and a refreshed and invigorated body. When the writer complains of how sick his heart is, he yearns for some ray of hope. When he complains of his isolation, he yearns for fellowship, companionship, and the familiar feeling of "home."

I encourage you to flip through the book of Psalms and read through some of these Scriptures. Identify what some of the complaints are in the text and then determine what the yearnings are behind them. This will help you understand the distinction so you can pinpoint them in your own marriage.

Here's another example. When Jesus was on the cross, He cried out to God with complaints using the words found in Psalm 22. Let's look at this psalm a little closer and examine what the writer is going through.

> *My God, my God, why have you abandoned me? Why are you so far away when I groan for help? Every day I call to you, my God, but you do not answer. Every night you hear my voice, but I find no relief. Yet you are holy, enthroned on the praises of Israel. Our ancestors trusted in you, and you rescued them. They cried out to you and were saved. They trusted in you and were never disgraced. (Ps. 22:1–5 NLT).*

The writer is specific about his complaints. He feels abandoned. He wants to be rescued from excruciating pain. He is disappointed because he has prayed and the response has not met his expectation. Behind these complaints is a yearning for God's presence and justice, as well as his salvation. However, the writer also praises God and appreciates Him for how He delivered those in the past who had put their trust in Him.

The writer demonstrates the power of moving between complaining about his condition and praising God for who He is, His mercy, and His grace. This illustrates how we can appreciate and praise our spouse for who they are and their gifts in our lives even as we complain about what we yearn for!

## MAKING IT ALL WORK

Let's revisit Karl and Millie's conversation in my office. I'm going to show you how they were focused on what they felt entitled to and how they could have practiced other alternatives. Notice the self-protective strategies they employed because they didn't think they were getting what they wanted. Notice how they chose not to exercise their spirit through this talk. Notice their lack of generosity as they listened to each other:

**Millie:** "Karl, you've been working so much that when you come home you are emotionally drained. You are so tired that you aren't really present with me or the kids for the short time we are together at night. And then when we go to bed, there are times when you spend another hour or two working some more."

**Karl:** "Honey, you know how important my work is to me. Why can't you support me in difficult times like this?"

Millie started out well by communicating the specifics of her complaint without attacking Karl personally. She stated the fact that he is working a lot and speculated that this is exhausting him. She let him know she and the children feel his absence without blaming him. Millie didn't share how she "felt" about his working late. Instead she just described the condition, thus protecting herself from the vulnerability of exposing the emotional impact of Karl's absence. The problem with this kind of communication is that Millie is loaded with those feelings (thoughts trapped in the body) and is too distrusting of her husband to share them. Millie ultimately contributes to the emotional distance she already experiences with Karl by perpetuating the complaint instead of exploring a possibility for intimacy. The vicious cycle continues.

When Millie finished her complaint, Karl didn't acknowledge any of the specific content in the complaint. He missed the opportunity to be curious and explore how she felt when he takes his work to bed with him. He didn't acknowledge, appreciate, or praise her for her times of sacrifice. Instead he ignored her yearning to be emotionally connected, intimate, and appreciated as a friend and lover and he attacked her character by saying she is unsupportive.

**Millie:** "I do. I just don't want to continue this disconnect. I think it's bad for the kids and bad for our relationship."

Millie was getting a bit edgy. Instead of telling Karl how she is impacted by the disconnect, she just told him it's bad for her and the kids. She missed the opportunity to ask for a way to connect with Karl. She didn't ask the questions: What can they do to unite them as they were when they first got married? How can they rekindle the flame?

**Karl:** "I hear your frustration."

Karl did a great job in acknowledging her frustration, but it seems to be too little too late.

**Millie:** "Do you think you could plan your life with me so that we don't lose each other? Especially when things get busy? That way you would feel supported along the way and we could keep our relationship alive instead of putting it on hold all the time because you aren't present."

Millie did a great job by asking for the opportunity to plan together so when things get busy they can keep connected. But you can hear her giving way to the fleshly impulse to be right by blaming Karl for the condition of the relationship.

**Karl:** "I do get lost in my thoughts from time to time and lose track of what's going on around me."

**Millie:** "And abandon me and the kids …"

Karl started out taking responsibility for how he tends to check out, but he still hasn't really acknowledged Millie's hurt and feeling of loss this far into the conversation. Finally, Millie didn't pick up on Karl's offer or perhaps she ignored it. She chose to indulge her flesh to get revenge by attacking him. (She did this most likely because she hasn't gotten any sense of whether she has been heard or not.)

Millie could have stopped the attack and considered the price of her impulses. She could have then responded to his offer to connect by being curious about what he feels when he "gets lost in his thoughts." Getting lost in thoughts is not an accident. Maybe there are things Karl is afraid to talk about because he doesn't see any way through them. Maybe he is afraid he'll have to pay a hefty price for exploring those thoughts. All these things require exercising the reflective nature of our spirit to consider other options.

What possibilities might have opened up if Millie had first appreciated Karl's acknowledgment of how he checks out, and then reframed her complaint to describe what she goes through when Karl checks out? We don't usually think of appreciation in a context like an argument, but this is the greatest time it can make a difference. When we think everything is worthless, hopeless, and in despair is usually the moment we need to be generous.

This is where the rubber meets the road in a marriage. This is what Dr. Brueggemann referred to as "the thoughtful discipline of negotiation," the balance between knowing when to "sound self-asserting complaint and when to offer self-yielding praise." We are always negotiating our futures together, regardless of circumstances. And a person with a vision of alternative possibilities will not be held hostage by circumstance.

Millie made a poor assumption about Karl when she attacked his character by saying he abandons her and the kids. This just escalated the argument. Millie could have said something like, "Karl, I appreciate that you noticed that you check out. That makes me feel like we are connecting." At this point she could have stated the possibility of what happens for her and the children when it happens. "I just wanted to connect with you about how lonely I feel when you do that. And sometimes the children get confused about some of the things you say that don't make sense because you didn't hear the full conversation." Unfortunately that's not the direction the conversation proceeded.

**Karl:** "Hey, I didn't say that. You did!"

**Millie:** "Well, what would you call it?"

Karl clarified that he didn't say what she made up and uses sarcasm to remind her she made it up. By this point Millie's impulses were out of control and taking over her spirit. She wanted to gain control by punishing Karl so she lashed out again. When Millie used her complaint like a hammer, she created a sense of hostility where a sense of peace is required for Karl to be able to appreciate her yearning.

**Karl:** "Millie, can't you just listen to me for a moment before accusing me? I don't want this conversation to degenerate into a cold war or some kind of battle. I feel worthless when you talk to me that way. The truth is, I am drained. I feel like there isn't enough of me to go around. All you do is rob me of my life! You're like a black hole!"

**Millie:** "I thought I was your wife, your partner, you know, your soul mate. Whatever happened to that part of our life together?"

Karl did well by opening with a clear request for Millie to listen to what he said instead of accusing him. He also communicated his feelings for the first time when he let Millie know he feels worthless when they talk this way. He even communicated his frustration about not being enough for her. Karl could not, however, stay vulnerable for long and ended with an attack on her character. He basically blamed her for his condition, characterizing her as a "black hole."

Karl also missed the opportunity to explore Millie's accusation that he minimizes (when she said he was abandoning her and the kids). He could have reversed the conversation by acknowledging that. He remained completely detached or hidden from her experience. Karl only acknowledged her experience one time in the whole conversation with a simple statement: "I hear your frustration." Being generous is letting the other person know that you have heard them in very specific terms.

At this point Millie seemed to have just thrown in the towel and fired back in a desperate attempt to guilt Karl. However, even in her sarcasm you can identify her yearning to be Karl's soul mate. She ended the statement in a tone that blames him for the disappearance of the romance in their relationship.

**Karl:** "Millie, are you serious? What is that supposed to mean? It isn't like you have been my soul mate either. When was the last time we made love? I feel like you live by a double standard. You want me to be your husband, but you don't want to be a wife! Whatever happened to submitting?"

**Millie:** "What are you talking about? When you say things like that, I feel like all I am to you is a commodity. Jesus never forces the church to submit. It is done out of reverence and love. You aren't listening to me, Karl. All you seem to do is think of yourself when we talk about this subject. I am going to take a breather and stop this before we say things that will hurt each other more than we have already!"

In the end Karl finally asked some questions, but he wasn't really interested in exploring. He used them as a tee-up for his accusations toward Millie and what he feels she owes him for his hard work. He reduced their sex life to a commodity that he deserves because of his status of being her husband.

Millie regained some sense of control and declared a time-out … while reiterating how little she felt listened to. She left the room and said she was doing so to stop them from hurting each other. It's like a final stab at maintaining some dignity before she walked out to regain her composure.

Both Millie and Karl got captured by the impulsive desires of their flesh, enough that it eventually robbed them of the possibility of connecting. Othering was not a possibility because of how they viewed each other. By the end of the conversation, they were both back to being the perpetual customer deeply dissatisfied and full of contempt for how they were treated by the other. They were stuffed with the kind of complaint directed at making a service provider pay for not living up to their expectations.

I record most of my coaching conversations to help my clients with the kind of forensics I have done here. When I played this conversation back to Karl and Millie, we dissected their statements as I have just done for you. This couple was exciting to work with because they quickly and easily began to connect to the idea that they could suspend their flesh to impulsively defend themselves and exercise their spirit to listen generously. Seeing the yearning behind the other's complaints opened their eyes to a new life together.

## SO MUCH MORE AVAILABLE

A couple of months after Karl and Millie had completed their coaching sessions, I received a letter from Karl. You can see the evidence of transformation that occurred in their marriage. It read:

*Dear Dan,*

*Who would have known that there was so much available for us the day we walked into your office. Honestly, I was in deep despair about ever having the kind of relationship I believed was possible when I first met Millie. Since our coaching sessions so much has happened.*

*1. Millie and I have developed a game we play with one another to sharpen our listening skills. When we hear somebody complain or we come up with a complaint ourselves, we write it down. When we have coffee together or at night after the kids are in bed, we pull out our list and identify the terms of the complaint and the yearning embedded in that complaint. It is amazing how we have transformed our individual experiences of listening to each other ... from resisting what is being said to being extremely curious and many times even excited about listening to a complaint!*

*2. Complaining without attacking each other has made it possible for us to talk about issues we would never have considered discussing prior to learning this discipline! In fact we have had a couple of difficult but rewarding conversations about the promise we made to each other many years ago to revisit the countries we spent time in with YWAM. We are leaving for Italy next week and will visit Jakarta in the fall.*

*3. Praising what we truly appreciate about one another during a difficult conversation is becoming more and more automatic for us. I feel like I am reminding my flesh that Millie is so much more than just a commodity designed to meet its impulse desires. I find that I have more room to reflect on other alternatives when I remember that.*

*4. One of the best ways you helped us learn to de-escalate a conversation was asking each other to clarify or say more about what it is they are complaining about. Practicing this has really helped me connect with Millie. She is such a gift to me! As I have been clarifying what I heard her say, it has created so much more room for her to hear me. I guess that is the result of generosity. Like the Scripture says, "We reap what we sow!"*

*5. Finally, when we first started talking about consumer thinking versus kingdom thinking, I was offended. I thought to myself, "Hey, I was a missionary for YWAM! Who does this guy think he is accusing me of such a thing?" I couldn't stop thinking about that conversation and in that first week I was amazed to see how I commoditized my wife, children, and friends to meet certain impulse needs. Then Millie asked me to consider that you never accused us of anything. In fact she reminded me that you had said that we were born into it and that all of us are influenced by it, like fish are influenced by the quality of water in their fish tank. It has been instructive to notice how often I invent being accused and blamed you for something when it may never have been said. We are truly*

*enjoying exploring the many conversations that seem*
*to creep into our minds.*

Karl and Millie practiced othering particularly in how they listened generously to one another, especially in difficult conversations. They gave to one another not only by listening to the content of what was said, but by asking each other to say more about issues that may not have been fully explored prior to asking that question. Listening generously is a perishable skill that can diminish if not practiced; however, it can also be developed just like a muscle when used in the best possible ways over and over again.

What is the best place to practice othering? Usually it's where you normally don't want to go—the tough conversations. I call those talks the places of conflict. I'm sure you know what they are for you and your spouse. Though painful, you must purposely voyage to those tender conversations. I believe it is only in that place where you can learn to reinvent your marriage and rewrite the *User's Guide* uniquely for the two of you. It is only in that place where you can rekindle your romance, your vision as a couple, as well as your faith in God.

## HIGHLIGHTS

- When we feel entitled to particular things in our marriage that we don't get, we use self-protective strategies to protect ourselves: We hide from, blame, or attack our spouse.

- The solution is to other. To other is to love your spouse by willing their good. We love ourselves best when we love the other first.

- Othering can be a challenge because it is a spiritual practice and our flesh and spirit are always at war. In order to exercise othering, we must daily submit ourselves to the Spirit and crucify our flesh.

- Listening generously to our spouse helps to control our fleshly impulses. We look past the complaint of the other and see the yearning behind it. This leads to a better understanding of where our spouse is coming from and powerfully unites us even in trying circumstances.

Chapter Four

# WELCOME TO THE
# UNPRECEDENTED

Breath of Heaven, lighten my darkness,
pour over me your holiness, for you are holy ...
*Amy Grant and Chris Eaton*

I want to toast my good friend Amy," my mother said, lifting her champagne glass high.

Hearing her words, everyone in the living room turned toward her, and the boisterous conversations stilled to silence. "To Amy," Mom continued on with unedited spontaneity. "Thank you for the love that you have given to me and this family. You are a dear friend!"

As Mom spoke, I heard something that I had never heard before. It was the sound of my father heaving in sobs. Sitting at the fireplace, surrounded by his children and grandchildren, Dad wept with uncontrolled tears. All of us watched in silence as my seventy-two-year-old father cried from the bottom of his soul like a river set free. None of us dared to interrupt the holy beauty that had encompassed us. As Dad cried, I glanced at Mom and a wave of peace swept over me. I felt the depths of what was transpiring before our eyes.

You see, when my parents divorced more than three decades prior, it was a very painful and bitter experience. Even though they shared four kids together, they didn't even try to be cordial to one another. There was much coldness between them and it hurt my siblings and me to witness and be a part of it. When my father broke down and cried that evening, I caught a glimpse of the suffering he had gone through all those years because of his own failures and how he had harshly judged himself in the breaking apart of the marriage.

After the divorce my father spent about ten years in a state of confusion. He dated various women but wandered from relationship to relationship without committing himself to anyone in particular. During that time he floundered in his personal life and business affairs like a batter on his third strike. As he would admit himself, Dad was a mess until the day he met Amy.

Amy is a special person. She is a pretty woman with brown eyes, jet black hair, and olive skin. She looks like she could be my sister. In fact her family roots go back to the same village in Italy as ours does. Amy is clear and direct, modest and sometimes even bashful. She hates drawing attention to herself and derives great joy in being hospitable. With an impeccable eye for detail, she rarely misses anything and so is keenly aware of what is happening with others around her.

As Amy and my father's relationship turned into marriage, Dad's life came out of confusion. With Amy's encouragement he began to reach into the broken places that had formed with us kids and even with our mom. She was relentless in her quest to bring our family out of the valley of bitterness, estrangement, and resentment, even in light of what could be deemed an awkward situation. Amy even pursued and developed a deep friendship with my mother, making sure that Mom was included in anything special such as holidays or other celebratory events.

Amy and Dad had a child of their own, Giancarlo, and adopted a young orphan girl from Russia, who is now my sister Alisa. Their stand for family gradually took root as a legacy in all our lives. Through small acts of kindness, honor, and inclusion, the dividing lines between Amy's family and ours disappeared completely. The Tocchini family grew larger and we got to know Amy's parents, Virginia and Tony.

When Tony died a few years ago, I remember being surprised at the depth of my mourning over his loss. The mourning I experienced produced a deep love and appreciation for Virginia and her children, and she became one of my favorite people in the world. Go figure. It was strange but true—my father's mother-in-law was one of my most cherished friends. It was no surprise that my grief over her passing was overwhelming.

Twenty years after my parents' bitter divorce, we were a family once again, though much bigger and different this time. Now the Tocchini family was a mixed clan of disparate people—husbands, wives, children, half-sisters, half-brothers, grandparents, and parents—all reconciled under that one name. Through my father's tears the presence of the Holy Spirit came and dwelt among us. Through the humility of a genuine toast of love and appreciation, the broken places in my father's heart were healing and his days of mourning were transforming into days of joy.

When my mother finished her toast, and conversations resumed and dessert was passed around the dinner table, I thought about the creator of love, Love Himself, God. I silently wondered, *Who is He who is Love? Who is this Breath of Heaven who has breathed new life into my family? Who is this Presence who has touched us with such eternal kindness, allowing us to reinvent our lives together in the land of shadows?*

Amid my musings I watched the fire burn in the fireplace. Throwing in another log, I sat still and watched the dancing shadows cast by the flames. These shadows, although beautiful, were merely silhouettes of the real flame. A thought came to my mind. Perhaps this is also the way of love here on earth. Maybe what we know as love is a mere shadow of Love. Although we feel the undeniable reality of Love's calling upon us, as shadows of the flame, there is something more beyond this silhouette. More than what we can imagine.

God didn't rehabilitate our family, He reinvented it. He didn't bring it back to a state it had once been in, He recreated it into something unprecedented. And this is precisely what He desires to do with your family, with your marriage, but it requires that you stop and listen to the prompting of God in your lives, the one who seeks to reconcile your pains, mistakes, and burdens in Him.

In the depths of our hearts, even in the shaky ground of a crumbling marriage, there is a yearning in all of us for Love to do His work. To perform the inconceivable. To reconcile even the most distant of relationships. To bring us home to Himself by giving us the courage to go boldly into the center of the pain, like my mother, Amy, and my father did.

## RECONCILIATION AS A MINISTRY

There are broken places in all our marriages. They are birthed out of the conversations we fear to have with our spouse because they make us vulnerable to pain, ruin, and loss. These talks can be about anything—finances, emotional absenteeism, a rebellious child, an extramarital affair. They demand the power of God's intervention or they will slowly but surely chip away at the health and well-being of our marriage.

Much hope can be found in broken places because God can use those areas to reconcile us with our spouse and reinvent our marriage. How? Jesus commanded us to love our neighbor as ourselves (see Matt. 22:39). Paul offered love as the most excellent way (see 1 Cor. 12:31). This kingdom-oriented love that Jesus advocates is very different than the romantic sentiments often pictured in Hollywood movies or TV shows. The love Jesus has for us, the love He came to this earth to make available for us to experience and emulate, is sacrificial. "This is the kind of love we are talking about—not that we once upon a time loved God, but that he loved us and sent his Son as a sacrifice to clear away our sins and the damage they've done to our relationship with God" (1 John 4:9–10 MSG).

Jesus gave His entire life to reconciling us to God. He came to end the divorce between God and humankind and reconnect the two in an eternal relationship. In doing this, He gives us the same ministry of reconciliation. Jesus made it possible for us to be, as it is framed in 2 Corinthians, ambassadors in His family business, reconciling everything to God:

> So from now on we regard no one from a worldly
> point of view. Though we once regarded Christ in

*this way, we do so no longer. Therefore, if anyone is in Christ, he is a new creation; the old has gone, the new has come! All this is from God, who reconciled us to himself through Christ and gave us the ministry of reconciliation: that God was reconciling the world to himself in Christ, not counting men's sins against them. And he has committed to us the message of reconciliation. We are therefore Christ's ambassadors, as though God were making his appeal through us. We implore you on Christ's behalf: Be reconciled to God. (2 Cor. 5:16–20)*

In the New Testament two Greek words, *apokatallasso* and *katallasso,* are translated as the English verb "to reconcile." Both words have similar meanings: *katallasso* is "to set up a relationship of peace not existing before" as in God reconciling man to Himself, and *apokatallasso* means "to restore a relationship of peace that has been disturbed."[1] I like a definition of *peace* I recently read—"the tranquil state of a soul assured of its salvation through Christ, fearing nothing from God and consequently content with its earthly lot, whatever it is … a state of conscious reconciliation with God …"[2] How many of us want and even need to experience this type of peace in our marriage? Many, I'm sure.

## THE RANSOM PRINCIPLE

In order for Jesus to reconcile us to God, He had to give Himself as a ransom. He paid a price—His own life—so that we could have peace in our lives and live life in freedom and with great abundance.

In order for our marriages to experience a reinvention, we must be willing to enter the broken places of our heart as a ransom. I like to refer to this process as the "Ransom Principle."

In the Bible one of the first illustrations of this act is found in the story of Abraham. In the Old Testament, Abraham was called to sacrifice, or ransom, his son Isaac, the very child that God had miraculously given Abraham and his barren wife, the very child through whom God promised many nations to be born. (You can read the story in the book of Genesis.)

The Ransom Principle is the paradox of life in the kingdom of God. While Isaac was spared, this commission was a pattern God followed with His own Son. It is the channel God uses to reconcile friendships, marriages, families, communities, and nations. When we are willing to lose it all in a relationship to gain God, we have access to the peace of our eternal life now. We experience the kingdom of God on earth. "Whoever finds his life will lose it, and whoever loses his life for my sake will find it" (Matt. 10:39).

I have been blessed to be a witness to many instances of ransoming in our family. I have watched Amy ransom herself by actively working with our family in times of turmoil when she really didn't have to extend herself. She has risked being judged and rejected for the possibility of seeing my biological family members reconciling. Her entire relationship with my father has revolved around the Ransom Principle.

I have watched my mother and father ransom themselves by giving up their offenses toward one another to restore the peace that had been broken. I have watched my siblings also restore peace in our family by surrendering any entitlement they may have felt toward my father, or mother, or because of tradition for the reconciliation of the family.

I lived out the Ransom Principle in my own way. I remember when Amy began dating my father. I was suspicious of her motives as I found it odd that she was romantically involved with someone as old as my dad. The deeper their relationship grew, the more I despaired. For a long time I was unable to recognize how God was working with this situation for our good. Finally, I was able to ransom myself for the well-being of our family by letting go of my bitterness, suspicions, and my need to be right about Amy's motives. Had I not done so, I would have missed the beauty of our family reconciling.

Of course, none of this happened overnight and without diligent and courageous conversations. It took a lot of work for me to even acknowledge that a broken place as it concerned my father and his failed marriage even existed.

## BROKEN PROMISES, BROKEN PLACES

Many of us are quick to pretend that our marriages are conflict-free. Others admit to broken places, but feel they have been resolved a long time ago. I strongly believe there is more room for reconciliation and reinvention than we may think because marriage is a place where conflict is ever present. Disagreements always pop up and needs always go unmet. It is the basic nature of relationships.

Think of your marriage in terms of the covenants you spoke on your wedding day. Remember your vows to "love, honor, and cherish until death do us part" and "to provide nurture and support in good times and in bad"? These are promises that bind your lives by transforming a right you have to yourself into a duty you have to another person.

It becomes your moral responsibility to keep whatever promise you make. This is what it means to give our word. When we give our word to our spouse about something, an expectation is immediately created. What happens if we don't meet those expectations? Our spouse becomes disappointed. This happens frequently in marriages and is a breeding ground for broken places.

Sometimes we get disappointed by expecting things that weren't promised. This is why it is wise to account for our covenants in very specific terms. Here is where we can unveil false expectations and validate overlooked expectations that are legitimate.

Here's an example. Say a drug addict comes to her mother to ask for money to "pay rent." Aware of her daughter's habit, the mother denies her the money and instead offers to pay for her to go to a rehab center for a month. The addict is disappointed and, in her anger and frustration, attacks her mother for being uncaring and for abandoning her. The difficult decision to not give this young woman money for rent can be a fulfillment of a covenant a family shares—to not partake in codependent behavior and enable a family member in their addiction. However, in the eyes of an addict, it is deemed as an act of betrayal, not one of love.

A mother's covenant to her children is to love, nurture, and protect them. If she enables them to destructive behavior, she is breaking her covenant even if her children think what she is doing is wrong. Expectations of a covenant must be outlined or the parties to the agreement can get disappointed, angry, or even caught up in a cycle of codependency. We must be clear as to what we mean when we give a promise to do something. What does making a promise entail? How far will we go to keep the promise? You get the picture.

## WHAT'S THE BIG DEAL ABOUT A COVENANT?

Covenant matters greatly to God. The Bible, for instance, is founded on the principle of making and keeping promises. Think about the names *Old* and *New Testament*. The word *testament* "is equivalent to *covenant,* and in our use of it, we apply it to the books which contain the old and new dispensations, that of Moses, and that of Jesus Christ."[3]

How necessary was covenant to our forefathers' relationships with one another and with God? The book of Deuteronomy is a series of conversations Moses had with the Israelites prior to going into the Promised Land. The word *Deuteronomy* literally means "a second statement of the laws [covenants] already promulgated."[4]

Moses was diligent to make sure the Israelites were clear about the expectations they had from the covenants they had made with God. Why? Because Moses knew their propensity to become consumers and follow after other gods in pursuit of self-gratification. And he knew that if they honored their word with God and with one another, it would transform their relationships and bring them closer to God.

This is what Moses meant when he told them to

> *Therefore keep the words [promises] of this covenant,*
> *and do them, that you may prosper in all that you do*
> *... that you may enter into covenant with the LORD*

> *your God … that He may establish you today as a*
> *people for Himself, and that He may be God to you,*
> *just as He has spoken to you, and just as He has sworn*
> *to your fathers, to Abraham, Isaac, and Jacob. (Deut.*
> *29:9, 12–13 NKJV)*

The promises we make to our spouse are the guiding factor for how we live as our word. When we live as our word, we make the choice to will or to act according to our promises. Promise is the beacon that is designed to remind us of who we are and how we ought to be with our spouse. Even if we break our promises to our spouse, we can still live as our word by repenting of our sin and shifting our actions to move toward rebuilding that promise. When we do this, our marriages experience deeper intimacy, fulfillment, and ultimate transformation.

Promise has everything to do with transformation. In Deuteronomy, Moses described the metamorphosis of an isolated nation devastated by poverty into a prosperous nation with a God-summoned identity. He tells his people that through making covenant with God, He will become *our* God and they will become *His* people. What could be more transformative than going from a stranger or an orphan to a family member?

When I married Aileen, she became *my* wife and I became *her* husband. Danny is *my* son, Elizabeth is *my* daughter, and I am *their* father. If I refer to another man's wife or children as *mine*, it would be offensive to both families because of the binding that covenant has on our lives together. I don't share in the binding of their covenant and they don't share in ours.

You may think me drawing examples from Old Testament history may seem outdated, but the ancients can teach us a lot about our lives today. New possibilities for the reinvention of our own marriages open up by understanding the nature of covenant they shared with their own families and communities.

When God made His covenant with Abraham (Gen. 12—17), He ordered Abraham to quarter a bull and put the quarters on both sides of the altar. This left a path down the middle of the sacrifice. In those days this was a common practice used to formalize a covenant between two or more parties. The path was set between the halves of the quartered bull for the parties of the covenant to walk between as they agreed to the appointed terms. It was a symbolic gesture that meant each party was willing to be fully devoted to the covenant even to the lengths of being slaughtered like the bull, if that's what it would take to fulfill the expectations of the covenant.

It's interesting to note that when God made His covenant with Abraham, Abraham was never required (nor did he choose) to walk down the middle of the sacrifice. God was the only one to pass between them. God's actions demonstrated the spirit of His relationship in fulfilling His word to man. In this act He was saying, "I will be who I ought to be even if you are not." This was also a foretelling of the crucifixion.

The story of God's covenant with Abraham is powerful because it shows us the character of Jesus and the measure of His love to us. It also illustrates how we are invited to relate to our spouse and our marriage. We are called to live sacrificially, to honor our marriage covenant, and to live as our word in the promises that we make.

Sadly the consumer culture has adulterated the true definition of covenant. It has divorced the word from its highly relational context and made it strictly a legal act. To most of society the idea of making a promise as intended by God's Word is lost, and our modern lexicon no longer has a word that encompasses this beautiful confluence of love and law.

When we are stuck in a consumer-oriented marriage, we aren't disturbed by broken covenants. We are even less concerned with being able to reconcile the peace in our relationship if it will affect our need to be right, feel good, look good, or be in control. Thus we are doomed to the curses that go with breaking covenants.

Consider the recent mortgage crisis and what the consumer culture has determined as the causes and what it has dictated as the solutions. What is a mortgage? A mortgage is essentially a covenant, but that is not how it is viewed in today's society. The mortgage crisis revolves mainly around greedy lenders and irresponsible borrowers. Most of these people never fully considered the promises and the expectations that bound the mortgage covenant, so it's not surprising that the pieces of paper they were written on basically ended up being worthless.

More disturbing to me are the solutions that came in response to this crisis. The government decided to give the greedy lenders more money and call it a "bailout." Wow! They used the same way to get us out of a messy situation as they used to get us into it.

Isn't this also the consumer answer to married life when it gets tough? We bail out of marriage faster than it takes to say the words "I do." We make baseless promises without even blinking or taking into consideration what they really mean. We journey through a marriage covenant without concern for who we said we would be to our spouse when we became husband and wife. And because our marriage does not match a typical Hollywood romance, we think something is wrong.

So instead of keeping our covenant and allowing God to reinvent our union through our broken places, we call it quits with our spouse. If we are aware, however, of the importance with which we make our promise, we will open the broken places where God is waiting to reinvent our lives together.

## NAMING YOUR BROKEN PLACES

Let's do some homework.

Review your answers to the first question in the assignment I gave you at the end of chapter 2. Allow them to serve as a conversational map to expose the broken places in your marriage.

**1.** When you think of the topics of conversations you wrote down, identify the disappointment that you experience when having these discussions. What expectations were not met? Do you consider them legitimate expectations? What promises were broken?

**2.** Now write down the potential risks you feel are involved in having these conversations. What do you fear losing? What are you afraid will happen when you talk about these things? Maybe you are afraid your spouse will divorce you. Perhaps you are afraid of the damage that can occur in the area of trust. Whatever you write down is the ransom you could sacrifice if you have the conversation.

**3.** Think about what your marriage is like by *not* having the conversation. What *isn't* possible if you ignore the conflict? Who suffers? What don't you get to do or experience with your spouse and with God as a result of this broken place?

**4.** Now write down what you imagine the relationship might be like if you and your spouse successfully had this conversation. In other words, what type of future is worth the ransom? Is it a marriage full of trust? Peace? A union that is fulfilling?

## BREAKING THROUGH

Jesus invites us, "Step out of shadows and lesser things of this temporary world."[5] He urges us to choose life in the midst of what is horrible, hopelessly broken, and destitute in order to reconcile the conflicted areas of our marriage. He wants us to break through the barriers of fear that box us in and keep us from reinventing our lives together.

After nine years of marriage, Aileen and I were talking divorce. We had two children; Danny was four and Elizabeth was one. Aileen had started her own business and I was working hours away in San Francisco. Our marriage was dissolving before our eyes and neither of us had done anything about it to change course.

Up until this point we had only occasionally been willing to touch the broken places, but it wasn't an ongoing practice in the natural course of our lives together. I had kicked a seven-year cocaine addiction four years prior to this and had developed an intimate relationship with God. Faith was just as important to Aileen and she regularly prayed for our marriage. However, our relationship had fallen into a rut because we avoided conflict as much as possible.

We both navigated our discussions around the topics we so desperately wanted to ignore. Gradually we learned to expect less from each other with regard to the quality of our life. As a result of this growing apathy, we found ourselves isolated from each other. We had given up on breaking through to our dreams because we couldn't see the way toward them from the box that held us hostage. Like prisoners in a jail of our own making, we had resigned ourselves to simply existing in our marriage so that we wouldn't lose what little we had. The less we expected from each other, the less disappointment there would be.

We also didn't fully trust that God would meet us in our broken places. At the same time, we maintained all the trappings of the typical Christian family. We went to church, paid our tithes, attended small groups, and so on. We were going through the motions, avoiding as much conflict as we could, and not expecting anything new in our marriage.

Through his studies of couples, marriage researcher Donald Baucom has found that couples who have high expectations for romance and passion in their relationship are more likely to have these qualities in their marriages than those who have low expectations; those with higher expectations also have more fulfilled marriages.[6] Furthermore, Shirley Glass explains in her book *Not Just Friends* that when spouses avoid talking to each other about the deeper experiences of life, they put their marriage at risk for infidelity.

In hindsight, after studying what these two researchers had to say, it was obvious what was happening in my marriage. Avoiding conflict was only making our lives more difficult and raising the odds of divorce. Now, if you would have talked to me at the time, I would have said Aileen and I were happy. But really she and I had just found a level of despair we could tolerate and called it happiness. We were convinced there couldn't have been anything more than what we had settled for.

One night I was particularly lonely lying next to my sleeping wife. I started to pray for God to show me what was missing from our deadening relationship. I picked up the Bible and it fell open to a passage found in 1 John.

> *God is light; in him there is no darkness at all. If we claim to have fellowship with him yet walk in the darkness, we lie and do not live by the truth. But if we walk in the light, as he is in the light, we have fellowship with one another, and the blood of Jesus, his Son, purifies us from all sin. (1 John 1:5–7)*

I thought, *Wow! That is so amazing.* I want a deeper relationship with Aileen and God says the way to do that is to walk in the light. A brief study of the word *light* in this context revealed that it meant conversing honestly with one another and bringing the things we keep to ourselves into the place where others can hear and see what is going on for us. Though excited at this budding revelation, I went to sleep that night deeply troubled.

The next morning I woke and waited for Aileen to take the kids outside while I ate my breakfast. I sat and watched my son and his friend playing on my wife's lap as the golden morning sunlight danced on her thick, curly, chestnut brown hair. She looked so beautiful. I'll never forget that moment because I realized what I had hidden in the darkness that needed to come into the light—my infidelities.

My heart jumped into my throat and my stomach began to turn. All of a sudden the lethargy and apathy in my life disappeared. I had no idea how this conversation would turn out, but I realized I really needed to get real with Aileen and let her know of my sins against her. It was how I needed to walk in the light. I arranged to meet her alone that evening after work. All day long I had thought how I would frame this talk. I was frightened and sure my life as it had been up until that point with Aileen would come to an end.

When the time came, I started to confess everything to Aileen. She listened intently, and when I was done, she began to ask all sorts of questions. Who were the women? How many times did I do it? Did I carry on an affair with any of them or were they all one-night stands? Did I love them? Were they married? Did their husbands know? She hurled question after question my way and after a while I got angry. At question eight I stood up and stormed out of the room.

At that moment, my wife took the first step and gave up avoiding or hiding from the difficult conversations, our broken places. She began to break through the box our married life was stuck in. Aileen came after me and said, "Dan, what was your purpose for confessing?"

I stopped and thought about it for a moment and then replied, "I wanted to clear the air between us."

With a tenderness in her voice and with tears in her eyes, she said, "Well, I feel used by the way you handled this conversation. When I asked questions about your betrayal, you got mad at me and wanted to walk away. It doesn't make sense and it's not fair. The way you acted is what hurts me. In fact it makes me think you are only confessing to relieve yourself of guilt, not because you see how you have hurt me and our family. Dan, are you really interested in me or the quality of our lives together or are you just trying to feel better about yourself?"

As I listened, her words cut me like a hot knife. I remember my knees almost buckled. While she was sharing, I thought of how my mother once told me of how her heart had grown cold for my father because of his infidelities and unwillingness to be honest about them. Aileen's words brought me back to life, and when she had finished, I told her, "I am ashamed of what I have done. You're right. I am trying to hide from that shame. I don't know what to do to recover our relationship."

Aileen looked me in the eyes and with a clear and grounded voice said, "Will you ransom your pride for our relationship and answer my questions? If you want any chance of having this marriage work, I think it really depends on God. I know I am numb and need some time to work through this with you. I don't know where I am about all this. Will you please just answer my questions?"

As my anger subsided, a sense of grief and despair welled up and tears poured down my face. Aileen's words had penetrated the automatic defense I used so many times before in our relationship. She had broken through and I was finally connecting to the impact my infidelity had on her and our family.

I was boxed in by the "Esau syndrome" that the writer of Hebrews talked about as "trading away God's lifelong gift in order to satisfy a short-term appetite ... Esau later regretted that impulsive act and wanted God's blessing—but by then it was too late, tears or no tears" (Heb. 12:16–17 MSG). Aileen had graciously shown me that in my helplessness to change the situation, I was numbing out in anger to give myself the illusion of control. Basically I traded God working in our marriage with life on my terms.

If I wanted our marriage to work, I would have to ransom my need for a sense of control to connect with the pain I had caused her. She was calling me out from behind my defenses to walk in the light with her. While it was extremely painful, it was real. We were beginning to love each other instead of being ruled by the controlled convenience of our defense mechanisms.

At one point I asked, "Aileen, will you forgive me?" She paused for a long time and said, "I will. But I don't know what I am going to choose about our marriage. I need some time."

We talked late into the night and listened to each other in ways we had never experienced up until that evening. In our conversation I realized how deeply I had alienated my wife with my selfishness and, more than anything, I was committed to respect and cherish her again regardless of what she decided about our marriage.

In order to give Aileen the room she needed, I slept in a separate room at night and had no sexual contact with her. The process took almost a year. I am convinced that it was one of the best decisions we made together. I promised her that I would wait for her to decide how she wanted me in the house. We didn't use a therapist; it didn't occur to us. We involved people in our lives we deeply respected. My father had just married Amy and they were both a great source of love and wisdom along with a couple of key friends from our church.

Aileen and I continued having conversations from the broken places we had never visited before. They caused us to break through to one another in unprecedented ways. One of the most powerful conversations we had was around what it means to forgive.

## REINVENTING LIFE ON GOD'S TERMS

While exploring the choices we both made and the prices and rewards involved in them, Aileen and I practiced having conversations that we would normally avoid. For instance, we explored what the similarities in my infidelities were, how I was relating to her, and what made my affairs such an enticing option.

We also explored Aileen's complaint about my sin. I listened for and began to identify her yearning in the complaint. She longed for a soul mate that would support her, somebody she could trust. As I stepped back and focused on her, it enabled me to receive her anger and resentment about feeling used. It made sense to me as I came to terms with my character up until that time.

In our conversations we discovered how forgiveness is directly related to the promises in our marriage covenant. Forgiveness is one of those things that has always seemed very ethereal to me, like a mystical thing that just happens to you out of the blue. In my desire to reconcile the broken places, I began to study what it really means.

The kinship between forgiveness and promise is displayed by the etymology of the words themselves. *Promise* comes from a Latin root meaning "to bind by sending forth." This is similar to the Old English root meaning "to give forth" from which the English word *forgive* is derived. The Greek word for *forgive* has a similar meaning;

it is a compound of two words meaning "to send from." These similarities are not mere coincidence, but reveal the intimate connection between promise and forgiveness.

A broken promise that is not forgiven causes bitterness. Promise binds us to the future, while bitterness binds us to the past. If I don't forgive, my life becomes about seeking justice or revenge for what has been done to me. It doesn't do anything for the other person; it is just my life I am ruining. My grandfather put it this way: "Bitterness is like drinking poison and waiting for the other person to die." Forgiveness is the antidote for the disease because it releases you from the chains of the past. It "sends" you away from the offense.

Remember the definition of suspicion Len gave me in chapter 2? At the end of his definition he quoted a philosopher who describes the impact of suspicion on our relationships: "Nature itself when it has been done an injury, will ever be suspicious, and no man can love the person he suspects." Suspicion is a familiar condition that logically arises out of bitterness, and it is only through the divine act of forgiveness that love can take the place of that resentment.

Aileen asked that we search out keys to forgiveness in the Bible and explore scripturally what it would take to reinvent our married life together. In my research I found a passage in Matthew 18 where Jesus instructs us to go to those who have offended us and take our offense to them personally. He makes what seems to be a cryptic statement that struck Aileen and me because of the work we did on covenant.

Right after Jesus instructs us on how to handle being hurt by another, He says, "I tell you the truth, whatever you bind on earth will be bound in heaven, and whatever you loose on earth will be loosed in heaven" (Matt. 18:18). What binds? What looses, or sets free? Promise and bitterness both bind and forgiveness is what sets free.

Aileen and I continued studying that passage and read about Peter's question to Jesus. He asks, "How many times should we forgive?" and Jesus responds, "Seventy-seven times" (see Matt. 18:21–22). In other words, always. It's a continual process, not a one-time deal. Reading further, we read about the parable Jesus tells of a king who forgives the debt of a servant. After his debt is mercifully discharged, the servant later turns around and prosecutes another servant for a debt owed to him. When the king hears this, he prosecutes the first servant whom he had forgiven and makes him pay the debt back. Jesus tells us that if we refuse to forgive, we will end up like the first servant.

Together Aileen and I began to work diligently to release each other from offenses as we discussed them one by one. We understood that we would have to do this multiple times until God would completely clear our suspicions of the other so we could hear the yearnings behind our complaints. As each yearning was brought out into the light, we found ourselves weeping in "grief over what should have never been and was." We were also able to identify "sorrow over what should have been that never was." As we moved into these areas of brokenness, God was reinventing our lives together.

Think about the bitterness that has been created from your broken promises. Are you harboring unforgiveness against your spouse for something they did a long time ago? Are you being challenged to forgive them for a broken promise? Where could you use God's intervention to soften your heart and reconcile the resentment you may be holding on to?

One night as I prepared for bed, I noticed an envelope with my name on it resting on my pillow. In it was a card that read,

> *Dan, will you join me in our bed? I love you more than I ever imagined possible and I am grateful for the dignity and respect you have shown me through all of this. At first I thought it was a show because I had never seen you be so tender toward me. Time and circumstance has shown me your true heart for us. Thank you for allowing me the time I needed. Honestly, our conversations have opened my eyes to how I have made you pay for your betrayal. Now it is my turn to ask you to forgive me as well. Will you forgive me?*

I never got up so fast in my life, and I bolted down the hallway to be with *my* wife!

## GOING FORWARD

Aileen and I have worked with hundreds of couples as marriage coaches. We have written two transformational marriage workshops. One is used by The Association for Christian Character Development (ACCD) called "One Accord" and one we use in our personal work together called "Loving Out Loud." Our hearts' desire is to open an opportunity for couples to share in the powerful reality of reconciling the broken places in their marriages, as we have in ours.

When Aileen broke through to me and I connected to the pain I had caused her, I was staggered. We both knew that only God could heal this pain. We both realized it would require our willingness to be ransomed to set the other free. If it weren't for our children, we may have walked away from the opportunity. In hindsight we are glad we made the decision to trust God and walk in the light the way we did.

Many years later we shared a powerful revelation about our reconciliation when we watched the movie *The Passion of the Christ*. One particular scene leapt out at us like a search beam. It was the point in the film where Jesus has been beaten beyond recognition by the Romans in the public square before they make Him carry His cross.

His mother, Mary, is in the crowd. When she sees how badly He is beaten and broken and how bloodied His body is, the pain is too much for her to bear and she turns away. Dazed by her grief, Mary wanders down a vacant alley, remembering a time almost thirty years before, when Jesus fell down as a young child. She pictured how fast she had run to reach Him, sweep Him up in her arms, and care for Him.

As she is drifting down memory lane, Mary looks up and sees Jesus carrying His cross through throngs of people down the road to Golgotha. She watches Him cry out in pain and fall under the weight of the heavy cross. As He falls, Mary races to His side and reassures Him, "I am here. I am here." Lifting her face with His blood-soaked hand, Jesus smiles and whispers to her, "See, Mother. I make all things new." The fear that drove her from His beating was being made new by His presence there at the cross.

Like Mary, Jesus' words shocked Aileen and me and we turned to look at each other in the theater. We knew without speaking a word that Jesus was telling us the same thing: "See, Aileen and Dan, I make all things new, even the death of your betrayals." And, like Mary, we don't understand how or why. All we know is that He, who is the Conversation, is making all things new, even our suffering.

The difficult or conflicted moments in our marriages are opportunities to invite God to bring reconciliation. Each time we enter these broken places in our lives and reconcile the conflict, our marriage is reinvented. But in order to enter, we must overcome the cycle of the fear or resistance followed by settling for despair. Many times there are hidden needs in our lives—things we chose to ignore or may not even see—that perpetuates this cycle. In order to find out those needs, we must start digging within ourselves, sometimes even using our spouse's thoughts and perspective as a guide, to determine what is eroding the foundation of our marriage.

## HIGHLIGHTS

- Reinventing our relationships happens in the broken places, where conflict exists because of broken promises.

- The sacrifice Jesus made of His own life for humankind made it so our lives can likewise involve a ministry of reconciliation, especially in our marriages.

- We engage in this ministry by continually ransoming ourselves for the sake of God and our marriage.

- Only in keeping covenant and living as our word can our marriage be transformed into a new creation.

- Reinventing our lives together requires the constant acting out of forgiveness in our relationship.

Chapter Five

# BREAKING THE CYCLE

Our intentions tend to be much
more real than our actions,
and this can lead to a great deal of
misunderstanding with other people,
to whom our actions tend to be much
more real than our intentions.

*E. F. Schumacher*

Malcolm and Eva are a couple who eventually became close friends with Aileen and me. They came to us many years ago in a deep-set dry spell, unhappy with their seemingly boring marriage. I'll never forget our first meeting.

They often reminisced about their early years before they had children. While he worked as a carpenter, she completed her degree in fashion. Eva recalled how much time they had together in their Chicago flat. They loved to walk together early in the mornings and plan where and when they would meet that night. Sometimes they would eat out and go dancing, other times see a movie or a play.

Malcolm really enjoyed the days they both weren't working and could spend the time doing whatever they wanted. They would sleep in and go for a long bike ride or hike and then plan a healthy meal and cook it together. Preparing the meal together was a time rich with engaging conversations and wonderful memories. With deep nostalgia Eva told me, "Malcolm and I would eat late in the evening because we loved taking our time shopping, preparing, and cooking the meal. I had no idea how much that ritual meant to me until we no longer had that kind of time together."

That romance and freedom disappeared after ten years of marriage when Malcolm and Eva became parents. Now when Malcolm returns home from a hard day at the construction site, he is greeted by his two lovely daughters, Jean Marie (six) and Carlin (three), and his infant son, Joshua. Malcolm washes up, plays with his girls, and holds his son. While Eva makes dinner, he cleans up and spends more time with the children. Eva is usually physically beat by seven o'clock and ready for Malcolm to help her get the kids ready for bed. Eva says, "By the time Joshua is done feeding, I am already nodding off. I can't help it. I'm exhausted!"

Malcolm said his day on the construction site is a warm-up for when he walks in the door. "By the time I get ten steps in the house, Jean Marie is hanging on my neck, Carlin wants to hear a story, and Eva wants me to bounce Josh around. Once everybody has had a kiss, a hug, and a bounce, I take a shower, set the table, put the kids in their seats, eat, clear the table, do the dishes, and kiss the kids good night. By the time I get to bed, Eva is snoring and I am ready to sleep with my clothes on."

"It's quite a different life from just six years ago," Eva recounted with a hint of sadness in her voice. Malcolm nodded yes and gave me a blank stare.

Malcolm and Eva bragged about what a great family unit they were in, working together to meet the needs of their children. However, the toll it was taking on the quality of their relationship was obvious. "I don't want to sound ungrateful," Malcolm confessed, "but at times it seems that is all there is for us—taking care of the kids."

For example, Eva believed the kids should be homeschooled and so Jean Marie was just beginning her first year. This meant that Eva got up even before Malcolm to prepare the day's lesson plan. She then helped Malcolm off to work and prepared breakfast for the kids, fed the baby, and then taught school.

Consequently the couple didn't get much time to connect with one another on a physical level. They rarely shared hugs or deep kisses. Sex in the morning was out of the question. Both of them said that in the evening, sleep seemed to overtake them before they can even get to talking to each other about their love life. Eva hoped they would make time for each other on the weekends, but it never happened.

I immediately noticed that their relationship had turned into a kind of cat-and-mouse game. When Eva told Malcolm she needed him or longed for him and suggested doing something together, he automatically withdrew and said something like, "Eva, be realistic. You know we just don't have the time!" It was a vicious cycle that kept repeating itself. Marriage research shows that this type of cat-and-mouse game is common among younger married couples with children. Here's a look at the nature of Malcolm and Eva's breakdown in one of our first conversations.

Malcolm sat back in his chair shaking his head slowly and said, "Sometimes when I look at you, I get the message that you're ticked off at me. Your body is tensed up and you have this disapproving look on your face. Like last night, I was working on the carpet for you and all of a sudden you shove Joshua into my face. I wasn't sure what you were trying to say by doing that, but I thought, *Geez, can you just give me a couple of seconds to complete the chore you asked me to do before you give me the next one?* I was really frustrated!"

Eva appeared concerned, and authentically acknowledging Malcolm's point of view, she said, "I see what you mean."

Malcolm leaned forward. "When you did that it was like you were trying to make me feel guilty and—"

Eva interrupted him. "—I have been so impatient lately. I hate what's happening to me. I feel awkward sometimes when I'm around you. Like I'm talking too much and you just don't have the time or don't even want to hear me talk. I feel like a nag. It seems to me you feel like I overload you with the same complaints every day."

Malcolm looked pensive, replying slowly, "I see."

Eva's response was somewhat defensive. "So if I tell you about how I'm feeling, you 'see,' but otherwise you miss the signals?"

Working diligently to empathize, Malcolm finally said, "I can see your point. I'm not doing very well at paying attention to your signals."

"I know you think I'm angry when I'm really not, and then you get angry and withdraw from me."

"Yeah, you're right. I'm thinking, *What did I do to get her so angry?*"

Eva shook her head. "We are really missing each other. When I see you look at me like that, I don't imagine you as asking, 'Why is she so angry at me?' but as saying, 'Oh, she's mad?! No, now I'm mad!' Then my anger escalates because I can't figure out why you would get angry at me. Even if I was mad at you, why wouldn't you ask me if I was upset in the first place?"

"This all makes sense to me!"

"It seems like a catch-22. It seems that we can't discuss the most important issues in our relationship, like our sex life, without missing each other. It's like a circle of doom that we can't get out of."

Malcolm stared at the floor and said with resolve, "You're right. I feel stuck as well and I don't have a clue about how to get out of it. Whatever I do seems to backfire or cause exactly the opposite of what I intended when I opened my mouth to try and fix the situation."

Eva came back with a slightly critical tone. "When did we go bad? We wouldn't have made it this far if this was going on in the beginning. I wish we could go back to the start of our relationship and do it over again."

"I think I'm getting very cynical because we keep talking about the same things over and over again. My cynicism comes from not making any progress when we do talk, and I'm sure it contributes to the vicious cycle we get stuck in."

"Then why don't you do something about it when you notice you are being cynical?" Eva retorted in a somewhat accusatory tone.

"I honestly don't know. Maybe it's because I think I will fail and then you'll chastise me for it. Sometimes I feel like you want to blame me more than be intimate!"

## WHAT'S THE PROBLEM?

Malcolm and Eva had obviously oriented their lives together around their children at the expense of their personal relationship. The symptoms were clear. Eva felt lonely and isolated from Malcolm and at times found herself badgering him for attention. Malcolm felt condemned for his mistakes and so he anticipated her attempts at getting him to pay attention and withdrew before she had a chance to get started. Neither of them paid attention to what the other was yearning for, nor did they clearly ask for what they personally needed from the other.

One of the most common symptoms of a denied, unclear, or minimized need is an entrenched conversation. They always seem to lead nowhere except to further alienation. Malcolm was right. Frustration and ultimate despair is the result of unsuccessfully navigating these entrenched conversations.

There are definitely some positive aspects to how Malcolm and Eva communicated and how they related to the other. They did a pretty good job at listening generously. They were willing to consider their contribution to whatever wasn't working without contempt or too much defensiveness. They shared a real committed passion around the covenant of marriage. This showed up in how they cared for their children.

Because of this commitment, Malcolm and Eva had some fundamental conversations in place that were quite resourceful, even in light of some heated issues. For example, while discussing the "vicious cycle," they were able to talk about it in such a way that kept them connected. Notice that Malcolm and Eva didn't *tend* to use their complaints to attack the other, but to communicate their experience and describe what they see happening between them. Even though they could express difficult feelings, they also were able to hear the other's perspective.

Like many parents of young children, Malcolm and Eva didn't question the validity of their challenges, but they did neglect the needs that lay beneath their respective complaints. They had convinced each other that they were too busy meeting the children's needs to be able to take care of their own. They didn't consider that reinventing their own relationship could in fact benefit the family unit.

Malcolm and Eva's repeated conversation kept them from even seeking to identify what they truly needed. When we are not clear about our yearnings and complaints, there is no room to determine how they can be met or even if they can be met. It's a relationship stalemate. No one can move past "Go."

Do you remember when Eva said, "When did we go bad? We wouldn't have made it this far if this was going on in the beginning. I wish we could go back to the start of our relationship and do it over again." She was expressing her yearning for intimacy by wanting to be intimate in a way she reminisced them as being ten years earlier. However, her language didn't communicate the specific need and how Malcolm could even begin to meet it.

This just increased Malcolm's anxiety about letting her down. Eva's ambiguous communication actually reinforced the perpetual cycle, though that was not her intention. As a result both spouses felt frustrated about the problem. Although they saw the deteriorating condition, they could not do anything that opened new possibilities to reinvent their marriage.

## SO WHAT CAN WE DO?

Have you ever found yourself stuck in a similar vicious cycle with your spouse? You know, those conversations that cause you to say to yourself, *How many times do we have to have this stupid conversation?* Most of us don't expect (and don't want) to have a difficult conversation more than once. When we do, we tend to think something is wrong, bad, or broken. I believe that when that happens, there are frustrated needs dying to be expressed. Eva and Malcolm's conversations were getting frustrated because neither of them really asked for what they wanted.

The key to successfully working through these conversations is learning how to manage impact. Managing impact means that you put yourself in your spouse's shoes and attempt to experience what they are experiencing in conversation with you. This requires you to suspend your personal agenda in the conversation so you can check in with how you are affecting your spouse.

Managing your impact is a very specific form of submission to your spouse and shows them that you are loving them the way you want to be loved. It is a powerful expression of othering.

When we learn how to manage impact, our spouse will see our willingness to connect with what they are trying to say, and so will be able to better communicate what they want. When people experience being listened to in this way, they begin to open up to possibilities they had previously ignored or resisted. The direction of the conversation is also subject to change and can lead toward a transformational place instead of a dead end.

By imagining ourselves in our partner's shoes, we can begin to understand what our significant other is yearning for. In the case of Malcolm and Eva, they both wanted time together separate from the children. If they recognized the limiting conversation that they don't have enough time against the backdrop of meeting their need for intimacy, they would be one step closer to getting what they both want.

## INTENTION vs. IMPACT

Is what we say to our spouse always the same message that is received? I don't think so. Think about your own conversations with your spouse. How many times have you said something to them, having specific intentions, but they heard you say something totally different? Did you get angry at them because it appeared they weren't paying attention?

So whose understanding of the message determines the ultimate meaning of your communication? The truth is that if you are committed to reaching your spouse, then what they receive is the ultimate meaning of your message regardless of your intent. Unless you are paying attention to what they derive from your communication, you will find yourself stuck in a vicious cycle of justifying what you say by defending your intentions.

In Malcolm and Eva's case, Malcolm interpreted that Eva was mad at him by her tense body language or the way she shoved the baby on him in the middle of completing another chore. It turned out that Eva was just exhausted from being with the kids all day and couldn't wait to get some time to herself. She conveyed her anger by her particular actions though that was not her intention. Because she was unaware of the impact it had on her husband, her assumptions of his reaction were based on her intention rather than her impact. This was why she couldn't understand why he often withdrew from her.

Malcolm, acutely aware of his intention to help Eva with the house, hid to protect himself from what he perceived as her anger toward him. Because he didn't investigate the impact of withdrawing from her, Eva felt abandoned and isolated and thus pestered him for attention. From his fear and anger, Malcolm could not begin to appreciate the yearning behind her complaint (wanting to be intimate with him). He only feared she was criticizing him, which reinforced his sense that she was angry with him. This caused him to withdraw further.

## BREAKING THE CYCLE
Malcolm and Eva's cat-and-mouse game frequently created cynical and fruitless conversations about issues connected to their intimacy. There was no listening for or expressing feedback about what each yearned for and whether or not the other could meet that need.

One day I engaged in a conversation with them to break the cat-and-mouse syndrome. My goal was for them to understand their needs through managing and exploring their impact on one another. Eva was doubtful. She relayed her frustration to me and said, "When Malcolm decides to talk with me, it's like pulling teeth. His resistance is as much a message as what his words say. He complains that I'm too intense! But it's the only way I can get him to recognize that I'm alive!"

When I asked Malcolm what he heard his wife say, he replied, "Sometimes it feels like Eva's so demanding it's difficult to hear anything. It doesn't matter what I do to help her, there is always something else and then there is the criticism that follows afterward."

Eva interrupted with, "If demanding to be with you, my husband, is an offense, then we have a serious problem!"

I noticed Malcolm beginning to withdraw from the conversation and I asked Eva if she noticed anything. She said, "Only that he is doing what he always does, which is hide in anger." I asked Malcolm if that was what he was experiencing and he began to break. Turning to Eva, he opened up.

"Eva, I'm not angry. I feel helpless and sad because it seems that no matter what I do, it isn't enough. In fact it just makes things worse. As a matter of fact, it's happening right now! I hate not being able to please you. Honey, my heart is to be with you even if what I have to say is difficult. Please forgive me for withdrawing so much. I can see how it's impacted you. But honestly, I'm not angry right now. I'm just sad and frustrated that I feel so helpless and I can't do anything to make this better."

Stunned, Eva answered, "I had no idea that was going on for you, Malcolm. Please forgive me for being so presumptuous. I can see how my actions have hurt you and fueled this vicious cycle. Would you be willing to explore more of this? I promise I will be more generous in how I listen."

Malcolm's ears perked right up and he sat forward on his chair. "Absolutely! It's funny, but I already feel like we are taking new ground in this conversation."

**1.** Think of the most common recurring conversation you have with your spouse. It doesn't necessarily have to be the one that's most heated, as you have explored in the other chapters. Write down the conversation as specifically as you can. How did the conversation begin? What did you or your spouse say? How did you or your spouse respond?

**2.** Now write down what you believe your spouse thinks and feels about this issue during the conversation. Spend some time on this exercise. Don't rush. Fully explore their experience as exhaustively as you can. In this exercise you will need your spouse's participation. Ask them if they would be willing to spend some time with you in learning how you can be a better listener in your marriage. When you are done, share with them what you have learned that you didn't recognize before today. How has your relationship been impacted as a result of what you've learned?

## RELATIONSHIPS *THE BREAK UP* WAY

In our consumer-based culture we don't pay attention to anything except our intentions. While we are very aware of those things, we typically have no clue as to the impact we have by what we say or what we do. Consumer spouses don't see any need to manage their impact by seeking feedback from their partner. They simply demand that they get what they want because "the customer is always right."

What is it we need to pay attention to when we are communicating with our spouse? Feedback. Feedback is simply the signals—including words, body posture, and tone of voice—we get back in response to our communication. Unfortunately most of us tend to deny the vital feedback we get from our partners because it makes us feel either inconvenient or uncomfortable.

The movie *The Break Up,* starring Vince Vaughn and Jennifer Aniston, offers us a powerful insight into the dynamic that occurs when we neglect the feedback that tells us of our impact on those we love.

Gary Grobowski (Vaughn) is a young entrepreneur in Chicago, who always insists on being right. Brooke Meyers (Aniston) is Gary's girlfriend. After an extended argument in which Brooke tries desperately to communicate to Gary the impact his way of being with her is having, she breaks the relationship off, hoping it will cause him to realize how much she means to him and his happiness.

The rest of the movie is a montage of scenes in which Gary and Brooke talk with their friends and family about what it will take to get the other one to change into what they need for a spouse. All the advice they get comes from true consumers, who give their idea of what Brooke or Gary should do to manipulate the other party to change. When they act on these suggestions with the other, each act of manipulation further escalates the conflict. Neither Gary nor Brooke accepts responsibility for the impact their actions have on the other and on their relationship. Instead they perpetually justify their stances by stating their intentions.

The cycle grows. Later on, in a conversation with her girlfriends, Brooke relates, "Not only is he out a girlfriend, but his life is just falling apart piece by piece and maybe that life was pretty great. And maybe I was the glue that was holding it all together. And if he wants that life back, he has no other choice but to change!"

Ah. Spoken like a true consumer. The movie depicts the cycle that not listening to feedback about impact can cause. In very vivid vignettes we see how each attempt of Gary and Brooke controlling or manipulating one another and defending their actions by their intention increases their alienation. The drama unfolds further when they each use other men and women to try and make the other jealous.

Finally, Gary has a breakthrough that turns his life around. When he finally begins to absorb the feedback of others, it transforms the way he responds to the people he loves. Gary and Brooke's relationship depicts the reality of what happens when we don't pay attention to the feedback we get about the impact our actions have on our spouses. Sadly it also represents the type of future that awaits us if we continue to refuse to manage impact and ignore feedback. While their relationship failed even though Gary finally saw the light, it doesn't mean our relationships are inevitably doomed. It's just a movie, after all.

Feedback is what opens our eyes to the impact we are having on our spouse. It is a looking glass into how others are experiencing us. Many people view feedback in a negative context and think it is synonymous with criticism. I believe this is part of our impulsive nature to want to be comfortable and undisturbed in our existence.

I like to suggest that every response or reaction we receive to our communication is a perfect opportunity to discover what our spouse wants or needs. Feedback can also give us insight into areas of our internal life that we may be out of touch with because the comments may not fit our view of ourselves.

If I view myself as a just and honest person, I will tend to ignore or rationalize the times when I am acting unjustly or lying to myself or my spouse about something.

In chapter 3, I mentioned a quote that suggested we view ourselves on a wide-ranging scale from flattery to fantasy. In my life I have found this to be a reality. When Aileen began to ask me about my infidelities and I got angry, much of my anger was rooted in resisting the idea of myself outside the flattery I lived in. I firmly saw myself as a man of my word, somebody who could be trusted, a loving, dependable, and supportive husband. When I was willing to get off my conceit about the kind of person I was, I was able to accept and deal with Aileen's feedback.

## THE FEEDBACK LOOP

**3.** Think of your own life. How often does the image you have of yourself cause you to turn a blind eye to the impact you have on your spouse? How can you better accept feedback even if it seems contrary to who you think you are as a person?

**4.** Here is another exercise you can do with your spouse. Approach them in a nonthreatening manner and ask if they would be willing to do an exercise in which you will ultimately listen to their feedback about a particular topic, without any input from you. I'm sure they would be happy to participate! The assignment will take about two hours of uninterrupted time. While it may not take that long, it's important for you to block out time where you can avoid any distractions. This exercise is designed to help you in asking for feedback from your partner. This means posing such questions to them as, "How did you feel about what I just said?" or "What were you thinking about this situation?" Keep in mind that this is *not* an exercise to resolve the breakdown. Its purpose is to hear feedback from your spouse and get a sense of the impact you have had on them.

Before you begin, here are some simple ground rules that must be followed:

1. Your spouse has full freedom to say what they are feeling or thinking about the subject.
2. You will not defend yourself or attack them. You are only allowed to ask clarifying questions about how they are feeling and what they are thinking.
3. When you are done with the exercise, you will not talk about it until you have taken the time to journal the thoughts and feelings that stuck out for you the most.

Before you engage your spouse in this assignment, write down two or three issues you two have that you feel are unexplored, sensitive, or even off-limits. It could be anything from a lack of sexual intimacy or your financial situation or differences in childrearing.

Some topics might take longer than others, so you might even just discuss one.

Now let your spouse know the purpose of this assignment—to use this time together to find out and explore their thoughts about some things you do not talk about very much because they are either too painful or awkward. Tell them that you would like to hear their unedited thoughts and that you promise you will not get reactive or attack them for their honesty.

Start talking about the situation. When your spouse gives you feedback, restrict yourself to asking questions about their thoughts and feelings. Remember the rules of engagement: Do not defend yourself, react in any way, or attack your partner. Just listen to the feedback. Immediately after your spouse shares, thank them for their honesty and let them know you would like about an hour to journal your experience of their feedback. After that time you will be willing to discuss it further.

**5.** When they leave the room, immediately write down what you are thinking and feeling. Do not worry about grammar, punctuation, or spelling. Just write everything that comes to your mind. You might want to use another source of paper if you have a lot to write. What are you feeling and thinking about the feedback you remember the most? What emotions did you experience while they were talking? How do you feel about what they said?

**6.** Notice how you feel after you write down your thoughts. Are you angry, sad, depressed, indifferent, conflicted? Ask yourself why you feel that particular way. For example, if you feel defensive or angry, ask yourself what it is you feel like you need to defend or protect. If you feel offended, what image of yourself do you feel has been jeopardized? If you feel you have been unjustly portrayed, what do you feel was unfair?

Finally, get together with your spouse to communicate what you heard them say and how you felt about the feedback. Thank them for their honesty.

Because we are human, we typically find it difficult to shake what other people say because it feels like they do not really understand who we are. We may feel like we have to defend our sense of identity so much so that we tend to forget about the other people involved in our discussions. We put so much time and energy in safeguarding ourselves that we become stripped of the power we have in transforming our circumstances. What does it take to regain that power and move on in a healthy and life-changing way?

## GET OFF IT

We all have our judgments. To judge is human and something we do automatically. In fact, as you have been reading this book, you have been judging it, me, yourself, and your marriage in different ways. I have been judging what information I should include in this book and how I should frame that information.

We judge so automatically that we tend to miss the powerful influence it has on our relationship with our spouse and the quality of our married life together. We form assessments, which is a form of judging, to decide who we will be and who others are and act from that place.

**7.** Some of the assessments that couples make can be dangerous and lead to a vicious cycle much like what happened between the characters in *The Break Up*. What are some recurring assessments you may have of your spouse that isolate, condescend, or put them down? What are some recurring assessments you have of yourself that may elevate your ego? Perhaps you feel that you are the hardest worker in the relationship or that your partner doesn't care about the effort you put into keeping your family together. How have these judgments affected the quality of your relationship?

A key discipline in being able to manage our impact on our spouse is to challenge these assessments. I like to say we need to "get off" them. This simply means we need to attach less significance to our judgments so that we can be open to truths outside of them.

Over the course of my years being a marriage coach, I have noticed common judgments among married couples that they want (and need) to get off, including:

- Successes and failures
- Agendas
- The past
- Comparisons with other spouses or couples
- Negative internal dialogue

- Unrealistic expectations
- Being liked
- Feeling guilty
- The need to be look good, feel good, be right, and be in control
- Having it our way
- Performing
- _____
- _____
- _____
- _____
- _____

Feel free to add your favorite flavors to this list as you discover the assessments that are barriers to intimacy with your spouse.

What opens up when we are willing to get off these things? Let's look at Malcolm and Eva again. I'm going to share a conversation they had after we explored their assessment that there wasn't enough time to be intimate because of the kids. In particular Aileen and I asked them to get off expecting their partner to guess or read their minds as to what it is they need from each other. Observe the difference in how they were open to new possibilities in physically connecting to one another.

**Eva:** "I've been thinking a lot about what it will take for us to actually have our relationship be something we cherish and nurture distinct from our relationship with the kids."

**Malcolm:** "So have I. I'm excited about some of the possibilities that have come up for me since then."

**Eva:** "Really? What are you seeing?"

**Malcolm:** "I know I am getting off of 'not having enough time' for us because I realize I have time to read the paper, go to the dentist, work out, and clean the garage. How did I get the time for those things? I made them a priority."

**Eva:** "What do you think we could do to make our relationship a priority on a regular basis?"

**Malcolm:** "I think talking to one another more often during the day, just to connect with where we are. We could talk by phone or email and especially do it in person when we're home."

**Eva:** "I understand."

**Malcolm:** "I notice I don't make touching you during the day a priority either. I don't stop and kiss you or just give you a hug. I do think of these things during the day and I'm sorry I don't even call you to share that with you."

**Eva:** "Yes. I noticed I wanted to hold your hand while we were walking home from the store with the kids. I'm not sure what I was afraid of that kept me from grabbing your hand, but I'm ready now to get off it and take the risk."

**Malcolm:** "Wow, that's some great feedback for me. Have I given you the impression that I don't want to hold your hand or be touched by you?"

**Eva:** "I can't think of anything in particular that you have done to give me that impression. It's more like an assumption that it would be misunderstood. It's a feeling of distrust that you wouldn't value doing it unless it was sexual. I think it may be just because we haven't expressed our appreciation physically like that for so long. I notice I am feeling very vulnerable even now as I tell you this."

**Malcolm:** "Okay. It makes me sad that is the case, but I really appreciate your trusting me enough to process it this way."

**Eva:** "The other day you complained that I don't like it when you touch me. But that isn't true. I just didn't like the way you touched me when your family was over for dinner. It felt awkward. You just came by and pinched my butt! I like affectionate expressions like holding hands and tender kisses. They are very comforting to me."

**Malcolm:** "Yeah, I even remember thinking to myself, *What am I doing?*"

**Eva:** "I am not saying I wouldn't want you to grab my butt, but when we haven't been connecting on a physical level for so long and then you do that, I feel used."

**Malcolm:** "I can see what you mean. You're right, it was insensitive and awkward."

**Eva:** "Thank you for understanding. What is it you need from me?"

**Malcolm:** "I need to know you feel good about me touching you."

**Eva:** "I want that as well. When you don't touch me, I feel neglected or detached."

**Malcolm:** "I didn't know that."

**Eva:** "Sometimes it feels like you are actually withdrawing from me on purpose. Is that accurate? Or am I just making it up?"

**Malcolm:** "There are times when I try to hug or kiss you and you don't pick up the signals. Like last night, I kissed you and you didn't even look up from reading Jean Marie's curriculum guide, so I interpreted that as you not being interested and unattracted to me."

**Eva:** "I didn't know that. I remember you kissing me. I can see how that would impact you that way. Wow, I can be more insensitive than I imagined."

**Malcolm:** "I need to know that it's okay to show you affection. Because after you were done reading the curriculum book for Jean Marie's lessons, you got up, got ready for bed, said good night to me, and went to bed. I felt like you were either mad or indifferent. Either way I felt neglected."

**Eva:** "I know what you mean. I laid there for a while really lonely and thinking it was too late to reach out."

**Malcolm:** "If it wasn't so sad, it would be funny. We were both afraid to reach out. That seems to be a picture of our relationship these last few years."

**Eva:** "Honey, I need you to tell me how you feel and to pursue me even when I seem to be distant. I promise I won't play a game. It's just sometimes I am distracted or not paying attention and your willingness to keep at it would really make a difference."

**Malcolm:** "I will do that. I think sometimes I am too patient because I wait too long for you to respond. I need you to acknowledge my touch when I do reach out even if you tell me that it isn't a good time to touch you. Will you do that?"

**Eva:** "I will. Just talking about it has given me hope for how we can be together. Funny how it really hasn't been about the kids, but about our willingness to ask for what we want. Our conversation has really made me want to make sure we have a night out together this week. You were right. We just haven't made the time."

**Malcolm:** "We seem to use the kids as a way to be right about not having time for each other and even for ourselves. Like a way to avoid having to do something about our awkward feelings."

**Eva:** "I'm glad we got off it, otherwise I doubt we would have had this talk."

Malcolm and Eva had a breakthrough conversation while in our offices that day. By being willing to get off of the assessment that having children didn't leave them time for each other, they broke new ground in their relationship. While the conversation was new, awkward, and uncomfortable for both of them, it brought a sense of possibility that rekindled their passion. They were encouraged by a deep sense of hope for what was possible for their marriage.

**8.** Take the time to journal conversations you have with your spouse that seem to limit your ability to be together. Conversations like the one Malcolm and Eva had about their children. They usually start with sayings like, "You don't help around the house"; "There is nobody we can trust with our children"; "We don't have enough money to go on vacation or go out on a date night"; "Every time we talk about this subject we fight"; "He doesn't understand how I feel"; "She is too emotional to think clearly about the issue."

Each one of these conversations represents a need that can be formed into a request. For example, "You don't help around the house" can be changed into "Would you please help me with the housework? It would help me feel connected to you and feel supported." The statement that "We don't have enough money to go on vacation or go out on a date night" can be changed into "Being with you is really important to me. I don't care if we go on an inexpensive vacation or date night. Let's think of something creative we can do together so we can enjoy one another and take a break from our everyday routines."

**9.** Form the statements you wrote down above into a request that you can use when discussing these issues with your partner.


## JUST A LITTLE PATIENCE

When Malcolm and Eva left that day, we encouraged them to continue to get off a couple of things. First, we asked them to consider the possibility that being great parents didn't mean they had to sacrifice their time together for their children. We asked them to consider other points of view that could be as true or even truer. One was that the covenant of marriage implies that they spend time with one another alone. This is part of what it means to "honor and cherish" each other.

Second, we asked them to meditate on the meaning of patience. It seemed to me that Malcolm and Eva thought patience had to do with waiting for each other to be somewhere they weren't. They thought they were being "patient" by compartmentalizing their affection when instead they should have been showing affection even when one was reading a book or fixing dinner.

I asked both of them to consider patience in a new way. Instead of waiting for what they perceived was the right time, patience was something more dynamic. It does not mean waiting until something happens over which we have no control. I believe patience calls us to live fully in the moment, to "show up" by being completely present to what is happening, to taste the here, and to be where we are. When we are impatient, we try to get away from where we are. I asked the question, "What if patience was that we persist in how we ask, seek, and knock to be with one another and with God?"

Several months letter I got an inspiring letter from Malcolm and Eva, stating how much more time they have spent connecting to one another on many different levels. I was struck by one thing in particular they wrote: "We feel like we are prepared for the next level of change that is undoubtedly coming."

Malcolm and Eva had broken through their vicious cycle by getting off some of their judgments. Their willingness to challenge their assumptions of the situations they faced opened new and powerful possibilities for them to reinvent their lives together. It also made them better equipped to deal with the inevitable changes that life holds. Change is a constant companion in this journey of life, but you're in it together … and that can make all the difference. There is a great temptation to view life changes as obstacles that have the disturbing power of shifting our world upside down. This is because change typically causes us to be uncomfortable and forces us to step out of our structured sense of living and, of course, loving. In a real sense, however, each new bend in the road is an opportunity to discover new and wonderful facets of the "other" that God has placed in your life.

## HIGHLIGHTS

- When you experience entrenched conversations, the best way to navigate through them is to manage impact, putting yourself in your spouse's shoes, suspending your agenda.

- The best way to gauge how we are communicating is to see how our spouse is receiving our message. What they hear is really what we are saying.

- Managing impact means exploring our spouse's experience instead of justifying our words, behaviors, and actions with our intentions.

- In order to successfully manage impact, we must ask our spouse for feedback—we must experience how they are relating to the conversation.

- A key component to managing impact is to acknowledge the judgments we make of our spouse and our marriage that make us view them in a negative light, and "get off" them.

Chapter Six

# WHAT'S NEXT?

Approach each new problem not with a view

of finding what you hope will be there,

but to get the truth, the realities

that must be grappled with.

You may not like what you find. In that

case you are entitled to try to change it.

But do not deceive yourself as to what you

do find to be the facts of the situation.

*Bernard M. Baruch*

The one thing we can count on in life and in marriage is change. It is constant. The longer you have been alive, the clearer this axiom probably is to you. As time passes, life happens and changes come. We get older, we get different jobs, we bear children, we move to different places, and we experience joyful and tragic life events we never would have anticipated.

Neuroscientists have discovered that how human beings relate to change greatly impacts their health, relationships, and their ability to creatively manage their problems. As we might expect, change is especially uncomfortable and distressing to the consumer who prefers things to remain predictably controllable. The consumer wants reliability above all else, having decided that they have "arrived" in their relationship. With the transaction complete, any kind of change represents a kind of betrayal.

When we have that mentality, we expect life to turn out the way we think it should and we resist anything that we feel contradicts our expectations. When we oppose or deny the way things really are, we are not trusting God or our spouse and become impatient and easily frustrated, a symptom of disorientation, which usually leads to a vicious cycle. We pull back from relying on God and become suspicious of our spouse. We attempt to find a way to avoid the discomfort of being disoriented by trying to control circumstances and their outcomes. When we find we cannot control anything, we disconnect from what is actually happening.

When we are no longer willing to be stretched by the changes we encounter, we cannot be blessed. Since change is a constant in marriage, learning to be completely present to what is happening to us while exhibiting patience keeps us oriented to our vision for a future worth having together.

**1.** Write down the kinds of changes that disorient you from your spouse—things like job loss, financial difficulties, problems with your children, the illness or death of extended family members. How do you handle these kinds of changes? Are you open to God using the ensuing discomfort to transform the vitality and health of your marriage?

**2.** In retrospect think about which of these changes brought new blessings to your life together even though in the moment you may have felt lost. How did God ultimately bring blessing you didn't expect?

**3.** Now think of the changes where you have felt lost and could not see any blessing. Imagine the possible blessings that could be in store for you and your spouse. Write them down.

## CHANGE SQUARED

There are two understandings of the word *change* in the Bible. The first is *metaschematizo* or "the changing of form, schematic, scenery or appearance."[1] The second, *metamorphoo,* signifies a divine transformation. It entails a "change that—under the power of God—finds expression in character and conduct."[2] It is the root of the modern-day word *metamorphosis.*

Changing a Japanese garden into an Italian garden is an illustration of *metaschematizo.* The appearance of the garden has changed, but it is still a garden. Another example of *metaschematizo* is how the apostle Paul describes his willingness to repackage himself in order to win those who did not know Jesus.

> *For though I am free from all, I have made myself a servant to all, that I might win more of them. To the Jews I became as a Jew, in order to win Jews. To those under the law I became as one under the law (though not being myself under the law) that I might win those*

> *under the law. To those outside the law I became as one*
> *outside the law (not being outside the law of God but*
> *under the law of Christ) that I might win those outside*
> *the law. To the weak I became weak, that I might win*
> *the weak. I have become all things to all people, that*
> *by all means I might save some.* (1 Cor. 9:19–22 ESV)

Paul's willingness to become all things to all men indicated that he had a deep trust in God to use his dramatic conversion and the ensuing changes in his life to fulfill God's plan. Paul's confidence in Jesus produced in him a transformation that transcended his self-interest so he could fully give himself to others. This trust is what made the apostle eventually *metamorphoo* into offering himself to the will of God. We naturally don't give ourselves to those we do not trust.

Our motives for changing our appearance are often about ourselves. We assign our happiness to looking and feeling good, being able to control circumstances, being right, or being accepted. We desperately scramble to look out for ourselves because we don't trust God enough to take care of us. This kind of self-interested *metaschematizo* effort casts us into the endless pursuit of more, better, and different.

Do these statements sound familiar?

"I just need to work more on controlling my temper."

"I want a better relationship with my husband than what I have now."

"I think my wife and I would be happier if we just implemented the techniques from this book."

"Surely, I can't trust God to work in me until I have changed all that is wrong in me."

In saying these things, we are seeking to move into a place that is more, better, or different than what has happened to us before. We are basing our present ideas and actions from assumptions about our past. Our history. What we knew then. What was true then. What didn't work then. And so we resist the ever-changing circumstances of life by trying to control them into past versions of happiness. Unfortunately there is no room in past versions of happiness for the type of transformation God wants to orchestrate in our lives.

Unless we make a conscious break from those historical assumptions, we tend to perpetuate only more, better, or different versions *(metaschematizos)* of what we have always had. We resist changing how we relate to changing circumstances; instead we just package how we relate so it fits our comfortable consumer mold.

I'm not saying that our past is a bad thing or something we should ignore. I'm saying that using the past to determine our future or to justify an unsatisfying present state is the quickest way to stop our marriage from entering into a new future, a future worth having. Think about it this way: While a rearview mirror is valuable to use when driving and you want to see what is behind you, it is disastrous to use to determine where you want to go.

## THE REAL DEAL

A future worth having demands a new way of thinking. This new way of thinking comes from the future and doesn't require that you "change" the things with which you struggle. It is a partnership with God to bring forth something unprecedented. This is what *metamorphoo* is all about. For instance, if you were to *metamorphoo* a Japanese garden, it would no longer be a garden. It might be a baseball field, a picnic area, or a playground for kids. It may very well still have the same elements as the previous construct, but it would serve a totally new purpose.

Transformation according to *metamorphoo* is dependent on God, not on our efforts. If we don't trust Him, we will never reach the potential of our eternal calling and will never experience a marriage beyond our wildest dreams. Make no mistake. This type of transformation is not easy. Often it is messy, uncomfortable, and downright tough. Why? Because true transformation is all about the death of ourselves—our assumptions, the way we think we should look, how life should turn out, how we think our spouse should treat us, how we and they should perform. It is about letting go of the need to protect or defend ourselves. It is about living purely from the joy of othering.

Instead of allowing change in your marriage to overwhelm you and throw you off track, you can anticipate it, embrace it, and deepen your trust in God to work things out as you give of yourself to your spouse. This is what creates the kind of patience in us to experience a future worth having. It even brings awe-inspiring moments in the midst of a challenging journey.

Trusting in God is a key to turning away from our defense mechanisms of playing it safe and heading toward blessings in the midst of life's changing circumstances. I believe this is part of what Paul meant when he wrote these words:

*I consider that our present sufferings are not worth comparing with the glory that will be revealed in us. The creation waits in eager expectation for the sons of God to be revealed. For the creation was subjected to frustration, not by its own choice, but by the will of the one who subjected it, in hope that the creation itself will be liberated from its bondage to decay and brought into the glorious freedom of the children of God.*

*We know that the whole creation has been groaning as in the pains of childbirth right up to the present time. Not only so, but we ourselves, who have the firstfruits of the Spirit, groan inwardly as we wait eagerly for our adoption as sons, the redemption of our bodies. For in this hope we were saved. But hope that is seen is no hope at all. Who hopes for what he already has? But if we hope for what we do not yet have, we wait for it patiently. (Rom. 8:18–25)*

## REY AND ENID

Rey and Enid are a married couple from Ann Arbor, Michigan, who struggled with problems that most married people face. They came to me disconnected because of constant battles over financial issues, the divvying up of household chores, a waning sex life, and a growing contempt for one another. The blueprint they had imagined for their marriage when they got hitched did not look anything like their reality. Rey and Enid were lost.

In our first meeting I learned that Rey had been a nurse at a local hospital for six years and had enjoyed the many benefits offered through that job. Enid worked part-time at a law firm as an administrative assistant. Rey loved his social network and living close to his brother. Enid hated the long, cold Michigan winters and wanted to move back to a beach town on the Southern California coast where she grew up.

Further into our meeting the ugliness started to rear its head. Enid said Rey managed the family finances like a kid because he was an "irresponsible spender." Rey told me that Enid was a miser. Their contempt for each other seemed to come up over the simplest issues, and they had plenty of history to support their accusations. Their behavior was undermining their ability to get at the deeper issues.

We learned that Enid's workload was increasing at the law firm and that at times it felt more like a full-time job. She questioned Rey as it concerned being responsible for taking care of the chores and their seven-year-old son, Micah. Enid remarked, "I feel like I have to chase Rey down to get him to help me out. I feel like a nag. If he cared about me and Micah, he would naturally see we need his assistance and just jump in to help!"

Rey reacted. "I work late at night, and when I get up in the mid-morning, I am exhausted. Sometimes I don't notice what I should be noticing. You could ask me to help you out instead of getting mad and taking it out on me later!"

Through their continuing dialogue, it was clear that there was something eating away at the foundation of their ability to listen to one another and empathize. The tone of their argument was filled with contempt, and it was clear neither of them had the patience to listen generously to the other.

At this point Aileen stepped in to shift the tone of the conversation. She asked them how they met. Rey told us they met in California while he was on vacation some twelve years prior. His countenance softened as he said, "We just hit it off immediately! We connected at a deep level and talked through many nights. When I returned to Michigan, we continued to have long telephone conversations and wrote passionate letters to one another sometimes three or four times a week. I used to really look forward to talking with Enid!"

Enid agreed in a nostalgic tone, saying, "It was a magical time in our lives together. Rey was so good-looking and so sensitive on top of that. I couldn't resist him. We got married four months after we met and I decided I could live anywhere with this man."

Rey did admit some initial challenges. "Enid is about seven years older than me and she is pretty set in her ways. She has lived alone most of her life. I grew up with three brothers and a sister and have always had roommates. So she and I have had to work hard on how we spend our money and how we work together in the house from the start!" Then the mood darkened when Rey admitted that before their son was born, Enid and he lost their connection and their sense of humor.

Enid agreed and began to emotionally break down toward the end of her account. "Not only have we lost the fun we used to have, but our fights have progressively gotten more and more vicious. I hate the way we argue and I especially hate how critical I can become. I'm afraid of what Micah will pick up from our example! I really don't want Micah to grow up thinking that women are nags and that he has to hide what he is doing from them. I want him to understand the power of being united as a family and working together. The problem is, I feel like I am raising two boys!"

Rey was visibly shaken up by Enid's words. "I have a difficult time when you talk to me that way. It feels like I am being belittled. I am not a child, Enid."

When Enid makes comments like this, she poses a distraction from a very valid concern: the impact on Micah because of all this bickering. Rey feels dishonored and Enid contributes to the contempt her husband feels toward her with her vindictive remarks. Rey backs off and shuts down. Together they frustrate their ability to get to the root of their issues. They get stuck on the surface of their lives, fending off attacks and positioning themselves to be right about their counter attacks.

"I know. You're right. That was condescending, but the truth is I do feel that way sometimes," Enid said finally.

Rey continued. "If we could learn to talk like mature adults to one another, Micah would learn what it looks like to resolve problems when they arise. I don't understand why we can't look at these conversations as opportunities to teach him what it means to love one another."

"That would be nice, but you don't do what you say you will do!" Enid's frustration was obvious as she called to mind the history.

"What do you mean?"

"Yesterday I asked you to pick your clothes up and you said you would, but when I got back from the store almost an hour later, they were still on the floor."

Rey's face had a pained look as he said, "I didn't know you wanted me to do it right away. I was working on a report for my supervisor and planned on straightening the room up as soon as I got done."

"You always have a way out no matter what I say. You say things like, 'Well, I didn't know you wanted me to do it right away.' It would be nice if you could just do it when you take your clothes off, then we wouldn't even have these conversations."

"But didn't it get done? And wasn't that the point?" Rey asked with intensity.

"Sure, but not until after we had a huge argument about it. It seems like a stall tactic to me. You finally picked your clothes up, but not until I did the dishes, went to the store for groceries, came back, and then put them away!"

"I already told you I had reports to complete. Isn't work and making money for us important?"

"Fair enough, but I feel you avoid helping me around the house more often than not."

"What do you mean? When have I done that?"

Enid looked reflective as she began reciting the record of Rey's wrongs. "Remember when I asked you to come and help me move the boxes in the garage? You were watching a movie and said you were busy, but would do it later. I had to go back out and unload the boxes a bit so I could move them on my own. When I came back in, you were on the phone with Mike talking about making a tee time."

"You're right. I did forget. Sometimes I forget things, but I wonder why you think I'm trying to avoid you. You could have come in and reminded me, but you didn't."

"Like I just said, there is your way out!"

The conversation ended with Enid taking some time to get off being so angry with Rey. His suspicion of her motives toward him has caused him to protect himself in such obvious ways that Enid doesn't believe she can rely on him to be responsible for anything, and feels she must leave.

## IT'S NOT ABOUT PICKING UP THE CLOTHES

Rey and Enid are suffering from a cycle of suspicion and contempt. They are also both asking one another for a *metaschematizo* change. When Enid says, "You always have a way out, no matter what I say … It would be nice if you could just do … then we wouldn't even have these conversations," she is asking Rey to change "how" he is talking to her rather than investigating why talking like that seems acceptable to him. When Rey complains, "You're right. I did forget. Sometimes I forget things, but I wonder why you think I'm trying to avoid you. You could have come in and reminded me, but you didn't," he, too, is asking for a *metaschematizo* by asking Enid to remind him of his responsibilities.

As long as they stay at this level of conversation, they will perpetuate the vicious cycle they are in and frustrate any divine transformation in their relationship. They will just find more, better, and different ways to make their points, make themselves right, deepen their contempt, and add distance to the relationship. They will stay lost.

I found in these types of conversations that the subject being argued about isn't the real issue. In other words, when things get stuck in a vicious cycle like this people aren't mad for the reason they think they are mad. Typically, when two people love each other, each party is interested in understanding what the other is experiencing. It's a natural expression of love and is what drives great communication. When that progression does not occur, I safely assume that what a couple is talking about is probably not the issue, but instead a way of avoiding what they fear God won't make provision for.

I had to work my way within these talks to find what the particular breakdown was.

They both said:

- They were far more connected before Micah was born.
- They were concerned about the example they were setting for Micah.

Enid said:

- They lost their fun.
- Their fights were getting more vicious.
- She hated how critical she could be.
- She didn't want Micah to think all women were nags.
- Rey didn't do what he said he would do.

By emphasizing these issues in her complaint, Enid is letting Rey know how disappointed she is in herself and in how she has been relating to him when they fight. She emphasized having to nag Rey constantly. Generally speaking, we nag when we feel we can't rely on the person who has promised something to us. This made me wonder, "How is it that Enid will nag, but not have a discussion with Rey about the way he keeps relating to her and why he keeps breaking his promises?"

Rey said:

- He didn't like being talked to in a condescending manner.
- He wanted to have conversations with his wife like mature adults.

Rey is more interested in being right. He doesn't explore Enid's feedback about her experience of him "being like a kid" to understand why she is impacted that way. He doesn't consider that he may be sabotaging the possibility of talking like adults by not keeping his word and demanding that Enid remind him of his responsibilities.

Gradually the underlying breakdown became clear. There was a lack of trust. Enid doesn't trust Rey to keep his word. Nor does she trust that he is willing to account for the impact of breaking it in a way that can produce possibility. Rey doesn't trust Enid enough to open up and be vulnerable about his mistakes because he feels she is condescending and critical. Neither of them trust God to provide for them as they take the risk of exploring what lies behind these obvious breakdowns.

## DO YOU TRUST ME?

Trust is one of those conditions we all recognize as important, even vital, to have a healthy and thriving marriage. In fact we decide to spend the rest of our lives with somebody because we "trust" they will maintain the integrity of the covenants that bind us to eternity.

To trust means "to place confidence in somebody or something as 'to *trust in* the Lord and do good' (Ps. 37)."[3] This definition suggests that trust is a decision we make, an act of our will. The last part of the definition also indicates that in order to "do good" to our spouse, trust is essential. In other words, if we choose to trust God to take care of our needs, then the energy and focus we would normally use to take care of ourselves can be given to benefit our spouse. Trusting in God is the fuel for transformation.

I truly believe that how we trust reflects how much we actually expect and depend on God to meet us in our marriage. We tend to bestow trust three ways: simply, blindly, and authentically. The first two manners prevent us from engaging problems in a way that can bring divine transformation to our marriages.

### Simple Trust

Simple trust is a type of naïve optimism that takes trust for granted. It does not deliberate or anticipate the possibility of betrayal. It, like a child, assumes an overriding goodness or benevolence in others. More often than not, simple trust is the paradigm in which most of us engage the world.

Because simple trust does not see people authentically, the conversation goes from "I can trust everybody" to "I *can't* trust anyone" when betrayed. Once betrayed, trust cannot be restored. In the case of our couple, Enid was struggling with trying to find a way to trust Rey again after he had betrayed her by not keeping his word and then blaming her for not reminding him. Placing confidence in him again didn't seem like a possibility because she hadn't really thought beyond the symptoms of the problem.

**4.** Think of some ways that you have trusted simply in your marriage. How did it ultimately benefit or harm you?

## *Blind Trust*

Like an ostrich burying its head in the sand, blind trust operates in denial, in willful self-deception. It refuses to look at evidence or the possibilities of betrayal. It anticipates the potential behavior of others based on history. In other words, the conversation creates an expectation that whoever the person was the last time is who they are when I see them again. This assumption causes a disconnection between spouses and a tendency toward taking each other for granted. Rey and Enid were willing to blind themselves to what might be the deeper issues as reflected in the broken promises and games they were playing.

**5.** Think of some ways you may have blindly trusted your spouse. How did it ultimately benefit or harm you?

## *Authentic Trust*

Unlike simple or blind trust, authentic trust recognizes the possibility of betrayal and yet still chooses to trust. Authors Robert Solomon and Fernando Flores noted, "It is wonderful if we simply find ourselves trusting in circumstances that warrant our trust, but authentic trust is that which trusts in the face of doubt and uncertainty."[4] When is trust more important than in a doubtful and uncertain situation?

Authentic trust is a conscious choice to give trust out of a commitment to the possibility of a future worth having. It goes into any relationship or situation with its eyes wide open. It is "both reflective and honest with itself and others. It has taken into account the arguments for distrust but has nevertheless resolved itself on the side of trust. Authentic trust is constituted as much by doubt and uncertainty as by confidence and optimism...."[5]

When I am trusting authentically, I diligently tend to my relationships because I realize that the trust shared is fragile. I honor the freedom that God has given the other person and I take into consideration what painful possibilities might occur, like infidelity or betrayal. Authentic trust acts in the belief that benefits reaped through trusting outweigh the potential cost of betrayal. Authentic trust recognizes anomalies in the relationship and investigates the context in which the anomaly shows up. Not only that, but it also automatically reduces the devastation that we can experience when betrayal does occur.

I invited Rey and Enid to consider the idea of authentic trust and asked them some questions to open their minds to this conversation: What was really going on for Rey? How was he relating to Enid and the family? Could his lack of sensitivity be a way to make her pay for something he wasn't even aware was going on for him? Would he be willing to even consider the possibility? Would she be willing to explore what caused her reactions toward Rey to be so "vicious"? What were her feelings telling her about how she viewed Rey? If she was getting back at him for something, what would it be? Would Enid rely on God if she discovered something she didn't want to hear or would she continue the vicious cycle by striking back at Rey?

When I asked Rey and Enid to explore the problem of trust with me through working through these questions, they were reluctant to move forward. Both of them became very quiet as they thought about what I had asked. Their reaction indicated I had hit a sensitive spot. Enid began to tear up and Rey was visibly uncomfortable. Rey asked me why I thought there might be something else to talk about. I told him that his excuse for not helping with the boxes and waiting on other chores over and over again seemed like a smoke screen for what was really going on between them. I told him that to me it seemed that he was getting even with Enid for something he was bitter about and didn't want to talk about.

Then I asked him if there was anything that happened before Micah was born or just after that he blamed Enid for that he didn't trust God, himself, or her to talk about it. Rey paused and sat quietly for a few minutes. He then questioned why I placed it in that time frame. I answered, "Because you both cited that you lost your sense of humor and things were no longer fun around that time."

Enid looked at me and interrupted my thoughts. "Dan, I think you are on to something. Before Micah was born, I was pregnant and we were afraid we couldn't afford a baby. Rey was seriously depressed and I was worried for him. I chose to abort the baby and Rey has never forgiven me for that."

Rey reacted immediately. "That isn't fair! I have forgiven you. What gave you the impression that I didn't forgive you?"

"Well," Enid began, "when we tried to have a baby again, I had two miscarriages before having Micah, and you seemed to get more and more distant from me. When I asked you about it that day in the park, you told me that you wondered if the abortion affected my ability to have a child. When I said I didn't know, you said maybe it was the price we paid for being so selfish. All I could hear was that it was the price *I* paid for being so selfish." With that Enid burst into tears and sobbed while Rey held her and wept.

Rey confessed when he made those comments he had been sad, but he had no idea that his remarks impacted Enid so deeply. They both agreed that they really didn't trust God to discuss this situation because they were afraid it would lead to even deeper rancor. They didn't trust that exploring and listening to each other would open up a future worth having together so they didn't want to risk going there. Ironically they were afraid of going there for Micah's sake.

Trusting God, themselves, and each other by venturing into that difficult conversation that day produced an immediate metamorphosis in the way they related to each other as well as their behavior toward one another. Rey asked Enid to forgive him as he could see how deeply Enid had been hurt by his bitterness. Enid asked Rey for forgiveness for her shame that showed up in rage and contempt. They both began to soften toward one another, and their levels of patience to listen generously grew as they explored each other's pain, suspicion, and grief that had been stuffed in their isolation.

**6.** Consider the areas of your relationship where you have pulled back or withdrawn from your spouse. Perhaps you have given up on communicating with your spouse and withdraw even before a conversation begins. Maybe you lash out before your spouse has a chance to speak for himself. Based on these behaviors, in what ways have you lost your trust in your spouse? In yourself? In God?

**7.** When did you start pulling back or resigning? What happened to make you act this way? Do you think you may have made up something about what happened to react so defensively?

Since our meeting in my office that day, Rey and Enid have been able to reach a much deeper understanding of what is required to maintain trust through the years. They have shared with Aileen and me how they continually ground their present relationship in the future they have decided is worth having together. The greater they have made the value of that future, the harder it has become for them to betray one another's trust. Still, they have not lost sight of the fact that betrayal is always a possibility. Rey and Enid are living a rewarding life together because of the freedom afforded by this kind of "eyes wide open" choice to trust.

## PRETENDING TO KEEP THE PEACE

Many times what takes the place of authentic trust in our marriage is what Solomon and Flores call "cordial hypocrisy." Cordial hypocrisy is pretending that trust exists when it does not. It is the polite smile, the corporate handshake, the religious nod. It is the subtle avoidance and the words of superficiality we use to hide our distrust of the other person. It was how Rey and Enid were relating to each other prior to their transformation.

I know of no better way to sabotage transformation than cordial hypocrisy. If you have a relational breakdown with your partner and don't pursue reconciling, then the resulting cordial hypocrisy implies that the relationship is really not worth having. With cordial hypocrisy Rey built a complaint filled with self-justifying rationalizations toward

Enid. Each time Rey encountered Enid, he pretended that there was trust, though nothing was further from the truth. Also, in their interaction they would say very little that was truly authentic because they both had already rationalized that it was futile to even try.

Like the tip of the iceberg, cordial hypocrisy is the first visible evidence of despair, which gives rise to moods of cynicism and suspicion that pervade our complaint and turn it into an attack on our partner. In this we justify withholding ourselves from our spouse and our marriage. When you position yourself to be right about what isn't possible in marriage, you throw out the chance of something unprecedented happening.

Instead of facing the problem, we run away. We use the defense of "I don't trust my spouse enough to engage in what seems unpredictable and potentially hurtful, so I will pretend I am *fine.*" Many times what "fine" really means is *f*rantic, *i*nsecure, *n*eurotic, and *e*motional. In this state of mind there can be no transformation (*metamorphoo),* just change (*metaschematizo*).

Any hope for reconciliation and transformation comes through our willingness to see how inauthentic we are being—and then choosing to be with the problem even when it looks hopeless. The best thing that can happen to us when we are playing with cordial hypocrisy is for God to expose what we are really thinking.

The paradox of God is that through us, imperfect vessels, He brings perfection. All we have to do is rely on Him. We live in a relationship, a partnership with the Eternal Being, who promises divine transformation. He can bring order to chaos. He can release beauty even in a mess. But we must first choose to stand and declare a future worth having in the face of the circumstances we find ourselves in.

Sometimes God helps do this using innovative ways and a sense of humor.

## CAN WE TRY THIS AGAIN?

In our follow-up conversations with Rey and Enid, Aileen and I had to find some ways for them to trust each other again. Enid was aggressive in how she related to her husband. She approached their conversations with anger and contempt. Rey was passive. He just shut down and became bitter at the fact that they could never reach a resolution.

We encouraged them to be creative in the process and introduced to them the concept of a "do-over." This piqued Rey and Enid's interest and they asked for more details. My wife explained. "The next time you find yourself starting out a conversation in a mean, accusatory, or unresourceful tone, one of you may ask the other, 'Would you like to try a do-over?' This is an invitation to start the conversation over and try again, this time using trust as the guiding force." Both Rey and Enid accepted our challenge.

In our next coaching session Enid recounted a particular event where they practiced this act of trust. Rey was out of town for a week at a medical conference. He was returning on a day that Micah was sick with the flu. Enid hadn't had time to clean the house; there were toys all over the floor and dirty dishes in the sink. The night before, Rey asked Enid to tidy up so when he came home, they could focus on spending quality time together instead of cleaning up. The next day, unfortunately, the house was in disarray. Before Enid had a chance to explain how sick Micah was, Rey initially withdrew from her. When she tried to talk to him, he threw a temper tantrum about what he had expected (and was looking forward to) when he got home. Enid felt her own temper flare, but then the thought of a do-over came to mind.

She told me, "I wanted to offer my trust and not indulge my impulse to strike back at him. I actually got what it means to utilize my reflective will and so I looked up, smiled at Rey, and made the offer." Enid started to giggle when she described Rey's reaction. "It was like watching an adult bear turn into a cub."

Rey walked out of the house and came back in five minutes with a huge smile on his face. He said, "Honey, I'm home! I can't believe how much I missed you. How have you been?" Then he gave Enid a big hug and juicy kiss. Enid returned the affection and described how Micah had gotten up at three in the morning, sick to his stomach and with a fever. She had spent the entire next day with him recovering in bed, as he was extremely needy and wanted her as close to him as possible. After the do-over a whole new resource emerged for the two. They had a great time together cleaning up, making dinner, and sharing an intimate evening.

Do-overs don't work all the time, but they do open the door to having more possibilities emerge from what might turn out to be a deadly conversation. I have seen hundreds of couples transform what would have been potentially volatile situations into opportunities to come together in unity. It gives them an opportunity to exercise bestowing trust on one another in times when trust is most wanted and needed. Most of all, this exercise helps couples not to take themselves too seriously. In Rey's words it provided them the space to recapture the sense of humor that had slipped away many years prior.

**8.** Set up a time to talk with your spouse about the most common ways you tend to harshly start a conversation. What are the trends that you notice? Do you consistently begin your conversations by criticism, looking at the negative of a situation, or being frustrated? Write these tendencies down.

**9.** Spend some time with your spouse to discuss ways you each would like to be approached when the other would like to make a bid for a do-over. Perhaps you want your spouse to give you a hug before he or she proposes a do-over. Maybe you would like them to do something funny to break the ice, like dramatically wave their arms around like a maniac and say, "Do-over, please, do-over." Make sure that both of you understand that the person being asked to do a do-over has the right to decline.

## THE NERD FACTOR

Humor helps us get some perspective about ourselves. It helps us rise above our foibles and lighten up. In marriage it helps us to forget about ourselves so we can find a fruitful and engaging way to relate to our spouse. I am a strong believer that God provides all the material we need for a good laugh in our own personalities. In working with Rey and Enid to develop their sense of humor, I shared with them what I refer to as the "Nerd Factor."

Most of us have a certain image that runs through our head when we think of the word *nerd*—an unattractive person with Coke-bottle glasses, high-waisted pants held up by bright red suspenders, and slicked back hair; a Steve Urkel look-a-like, if you will.

When we act as consumers and relate to our spouse based on our selfish impulses, we look pretty unattractive. We look like a nerd. Our behavior is so stupid, outlandish, and foolish that we act more like a cartoon character on Saturday-morning TV than a human being with a brain. Sometimes we are so wrapped up in our acts, that we can't even witness the absurdity of our actions.

Rey and Enid's assignment was to think of ways they might be able to laugh at themselves so they could be there for the other. They were to find their nerd. I asked them to notice the times they get so serious that they became detached from one another and more focused on themselves and their agendas. In those moments they were to think about (1) the strategies they employ to look and feel good, be right, and be in control; (2) how they behave; and (3) how comical they might look to the outsider who was observing their behavior. Then they were to physically exaggerate the main characteristics of those strategies much like a caricature cartoonist would do of a person's physical features.

This reminds me of a personal story in which I was confronted by my own nerd. One time I was driving my family somewhere and I got lost. I (you might say being the typical male) didn't want to admit I was lost. As Aileen increased her pleas to stop and ask for directions, I got more and more flustered and angry with her. My daughter Liz was about five years old at the time and was watching our feud behind me in her car seat. I kid you not, at one point she kicked the back of my seat and said, "Daddy, you're right. Now would you please stop and ask somebody for directions?"

Her timing was so perfect, and she so captured the character of my strategy in her innocent understatement of my behavior. She caused us all to laugh and especially made me realize how foolishly stubborn I was being. You can guess what I did next. It was a great opportunity for me to acknowledge and laugh at the stubborn nerd in myself and then focus on being there for my family. Because I allowed myself to lighten up, I was able to get off myself and reinvent the moment.

In our next meeting Rey shared with us his own nerd moment. By the time the story was over, I was in tears because I was laughing so hard. Rey had been out on a late shift at the hospital. Enid and he hadn't seen each other for some time and he was really pining to see her. When he arrived home, she was just finishing the dishes and cleaning up the kitchen from the dinner she and Micah had. He walked into the room, kissed Enid, told her he was going to clean up and then wait for her in bed.

With desperate anticipation Rey lay on the bed waiting and hoping for some intimate time with Enid. While she was brushing her teeth, he couldn't help stare at her beauty. With each passing moment his excitement grew more intense. The next thing he knew, Enid climbed in bed next to him, rolled over to kiss him good night, and said, "Honey, I'm exhausted. Let's talk in the morning." With that remark she rolled back to her side of the bed and settled in a fetal position to go to sleep. Rey told us, "I was thinking, *Talk? Talk? Who wants to talk?* I was thinking of other things, like some love, affection, intimacy, and, of course, sex!" Enid giggled as Rey continued his story.

After Enid drifted off to sleep, Rey dramatically sat up in bed, turned on the light, and began to read. Under his breath he commented how he needed to read some manual for work and he might as well do it now since he wasn't tired. This, of course, was a strategy he was using to bait Enid's attention. A few minutes passed and she didn't bite. Rey became more frustrated and anxiously sat up straight on the edge of the bed. He let out an exaggerated sigh. Enid stirred and asked, "What's wrong, honey?"

Hoping this would prompt some affection, Rey told her he had a lot of tension and couldn't sleep. Enid suggested he take a hot bath (it always worked for her), and rolled back over to go to sleep. With a resounding restlessness he blurted out, "No, I don't think that will work. I'm feeling deep-seated stress. I think I need some exercise." (And he wasn't talking about taking a yoga class, either.) When Enid didn't budge, Rey plopped back into the bed and tried to lovingly nudge her to get a reaction. Nothing. Then he got desperate and thrust his butt out in her direction so it bumped up against her. Nothing. Finally, he rolled over to face her and thrust his pelvis into her.

Finally, a reaction … but not what he expected. Enid threw the covers off her body, spread her arms and legs and shouted, "Okay, fine. But hurry up and get it over with. I need to get some sleep." With that, Rey jumped out of bed and indignantly shouted, "Is that all you think about? Well, I never!" He stormed out of the room, slamming the door behind him.

Rey sat on the living room couch for about five minutes, hoping Enid would eventually rush down the stairs. When it was clear she wasn't coming down, he was struck by another idea. He would leave. But first, he needed to get his wallet and keys, which were in the bedroom. Rey shot back up the stairs and into the bedroom, where he intentionally made a loud ruckus in a search for those two items.

From the corner of his eye, he glanced at Enid and saw she was fast asleep.

Frustrated beyond belief, Rey stomped out of the bedroom and headed for the garage. In the process he banged his knee on the washer. He started the car, revving the engine three times on purpose to make more noise, and suddenly he saw Enid. She was standing by the garage door in a nightgown with one hand holding an imaginary video camera and the other hand winding alongside as if to imply film was rolling. Ignoring her and too angry to enjoy the cute moment, Rey proceeded out the garage and down the street, without a clue as to where he was going.

Finally, he came to an intersection and set the car in park at the stop sign. Rey muttered to himself, "I'm such a fool," and turned the car around to go back home. When he was finally in bed, it was so quiet he could hear himself breathing. He lay there for a few moments and then this wonderful laughter erupted from his lovely wife who lay next to him. Rey began to chuckle and, before you knew it, both were laughing so hard their bellies hurt.

The next day Rey realized that he had always been a nerd. He told me, "I have run those same strategies to get my way from my father, mother, friends, teachers, and other people in an attempt to gain what I wanted. I have always hated to ask for anything, so rather than ask, I make my need known through what I feel is a clue. I make a hint or a complaint or I sigh loudly, and hope somebody will take notice and meet my need. Should they call me out on what I am doing, I will play dumb or reverse it on them, telling them it was really them not me acting like that. Then I'll likely throw a complete tantrum to get what I think I need. I can see why Enid gets so frustrated with me. I keep wanting her to do for me what I need to request or deal with myself, like remembering to do my chores. Recognizing my nerdiness made it so much easier to get off my need to get my way."

There is a nerd in all of us. In fact, if you are anything like me, you probably suffer from Multiple Nerd Syndrome (MNS). Do you know your nerd? Allow me to prime the pump by suggesting a list of the nerds I have myself or have witnessed in others. Picture a nerd in your head—with whatever physical attributes you so choose—and then as you read through the list, see if you can relate to the ones I mention. If you can't think of any nerds, ask your spouse what some of your nerds are. I bet they'll have a whole bunch for you. Write your nerd(s) down in the spaces below.

- The Important Nerd: being too busy to talk about important issues
- The Ego Nerd: building yourself up by putting somebody else down
- The Procrastinator Nerd: putting off doing something until it becomes a crisis and you have to get everybody who "doesn't care" to save yourself
- The Low-Self-Esteem Nerd: not "feeling" worthy enough to be with people and waiting for them to come and ask you to join them
- The Conceited Nerd: being arrogant to cover fear or insecurities
- The Fighter Nerd: attacking others' faults to put them on the defensive to avoid seeing your own
- The Excuse-Maker Nerd: trying to explain your way out of what you behaved your way into

- The Defensive Nerd: defending what doesn't work.
- The Bully Nerd: threatening to leave if you don't get your way
- The Blow-Off or Sarcastic Nerd: using humor to minimize a sense of guilt or to distract from discomforting situations

**10.** The nerd(s) in me is (are):

Being aware of these nerds and recognizing the absurdity that comes from acting out of that ridiculous place gives us a space to reinvent the moment. It gives us a direction when we get lost. It gives us an opportunity to redo a conversation that may have started out with criticism, sarcasm, or vindictiveness.

If you really want to have fun, ask your spouse to act out the nerds they have experienced with you. Aileen likes to make fun of what we call "Mr. Important." She will walk into a room like a king, sit in my fancy armchair, and bark out orders. At first I was a bit offended, but eventually I laughed, and today it helps me get off it quickly. My favorite nerd of Aileen's is what I call "Small Man," which I do by criticizing anybody that isn't like she thinks they should be. We definitely have a lot of fun with it.

# HIGHLIGHTS

- Change is a constant part of life. Don't fight it. It's inevitable.

- The inner change we need in order for a life and a future worth having is *metamorphoo*. To be transformed this way requires our dependence on God, not our own efforts.

- Authentic trust is critical in creating a new way of thinking and a new marriage—trusting God to provide in the middle of a marital breakdown and trusting our spouse, even when recognizing the possibility of betrayal.

- Cordial hypocrisy—keeping the peace to maintain a deadening or lessening marriage—is an obstacle to authentic trust.

- A do-over is one possible solution to reinventing a conversation that initially began with contempt, anger, or resentment. Try this at home!

- There is a nerd in all of us. Sometimes remembering what our inner nerds are can also help us to reinvent a moment and tame our negative reactions.

# CONCLUSION

You've come to the final pages in the *Guide*, and prayerfully a new beginning.

Now close your eyes. Take a deep breath. Think about your own marriage. Think about the twists and turns and detours you have gone through. Maybe you lost the excitement along the way. Maybe you lost the meaning or you've stopped hearing the Conversation. Maybe you lost the connection. Maybe you lost the intimacy. Whatever it is, I want you to know that nothing has to be lost. You don't need to experience a deteriorating or unfulfilled marriage.

Marriage can be exciting. Marriage can be meaningful. Marriage can have purpose. Marriage can exude passion. Marriage can be even more wonderful than you can imagine. Remember, God has an unprecedented marriage designed for you, if you are willing to journey with Him and trust your union in His hands. Be willing to be reinvented. Be willing to be stretched. Be willing to be transformed.

I pray that the ideas and disciplines in this book bring you closer to a future worth having. Don't get discouraged if it doesn't happen overnight. Nothing does. But over time, with prayer and devotion to your union, you will notice the fruits of transformation. And if you happen to be one of those happy couples who have not endured a significant challenge or obstacle in your relationship, I pray you have learned strategies that will keep you grounded, focused, and centered on a God-designed kingdom marriage.

Dear reader, no matter how bad your marriage seems right now, be encouraged. I am confident that if you continue to place your trust in God, your "us" will undergo a metamorphosis beyond even your wildest dreams!

# NOTES

## Chapter two

1   Martin Heidegger, *Being and Time* (New York: State University of New York Press, 1996), 288.

2   A. W. Tozer, *The Knowledge of the Holy: The Attributes of God: Their Meaning in the Christian Life* (San Francisco: Harper One, 1978), 2.

3   *American Dictionary of the English Language* (1828).

## Chapter three

1   Warren Wiersbe, *The Best of A. W. Tozer, Book 1* (Camp Hill, PA: Wingspread Publishers, 2007), 109.

2   Walter Brueggemann, *The Covenanted Self* (Minneapolis, MN: Augsburg Fortress, 1999), 1.

3   C. S. Lewis, *The Four Loves* (New York: Harcourt, Brace & Word, Inc., 1960), 121.

4   C. S. Lewis, *Mere Christianity* (San Francisco: HarperSanFrancisco, 2001), 192.

5   Dallas Willard, "Spiritual Formation and the Warfare Between the Flesh and the Human Spirit," *Journal of Spiritual Formation & Soul Care*, Vol. 1, No. 1, Spring 2008, 82.

6   Walter Brueggemann, *The Covenanted Self* (Minneapolis, MN: Augsburg Fortress, 1999), 11.

7   *American Dictionary of the English Language* (1828).

### Chapter four

1 *Vines Expository Dictionary of New Testament Words.*

2 Spiros Zodhiates, *The Complete Word Study Dictionary: New Testament* (Chattanooga, TN: AMG Publishers, 1992), 520.

3 *American Dictionary of the English Language* (1828).

4 *Easton's Bible Dictionary* (1887).

5 C. S. Lewis, *The Great Divorce* (San Francisco: HarperSanFrancisco, 2001).

6 The Free Press, 2003, 56.

### Chapter six

1 *Vine's Expository Dictionary of Old and New Testament Words.*

2 *Ibid.*

3 *American Dictionary of the English Language* (1828).

4 Robert C. Solomon, Fernando Flores, *Building Trust: In Business, Politics, Relationships, and Life* (Oxford: Oxford University Press, 2003).

5 *Ibid.*

**Discover More about the Author's Ministry Online**

WWW.ACCD.ORG

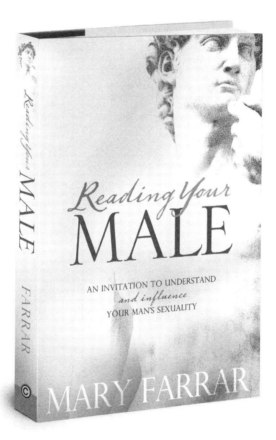